DWARF HAMSTERS

Judith Lissenberg

DWARF HAMSTERS

REBO
PUBLISHERS

© 2003 Zuid Boekprodukties
© 2006 Rebo Publishers

Text and photographs: Judith Lissenberg
Cover design: Artedit s.r.o., Prague, The Czech Republic
Typesetting and pre-press services: Artedit s.r.o., Prague, The Czech Republic

ISBN 13: 978-90-366-1551-8
ISBN 10: 90-366-1551-8

CONTENTS

1 DESCRIPTION OF THE DWARF HAMSTER

The rodent family

The dwarf hamster has developed during the past 25 years into a very popular member of the small rodent family. Besides hamsters, this family also includes the tame rats, mice and gerbils. The dwarf hamster belongs to the order of the rodents or Rodentia. The rodents form a large group in the animal kingdom, because they comprise half of all of the world's mammals. There are about 1800 rodent species, which have as a common characteristic two strikingly large incisors in both the upper and the lower jaw. The word "rodentia" is incidentally derived from the Latin word "*rodere*," meaning "to gnaw." The South American Capybara, which weighs several dozen kilos, is the largest rodent, and the harvest mouse is the smallest. This little animal weighs only a couple of grams.

What is a dwarf hamster

There are dozens of species of hamsters. A well-known relative of the dwarf hamster is the oversized common or wild hamster *(Cricetus cricetus)*, which lives only in the wild. This animal can still be found sporadically in certain parts of Europe. An adult common hamster is roughly the

Rodents have conspicuously large incisors; these are the teeth of a musk rat

Russian dwarf hamster with the much larger Syrian golden hamster

size of a guinea pig. The best-known hamster species is undoubtedly the Syrian or golden hamster *(Mesocricetus auratus)*, which like the dwarf hamster is a popular pet. Because both the Syrian hamster and the dwarf hamsters are widely kept as domestic pets, some people think that these animal species can be handled and cared for in the same manner. But a dwarf hamster is not a miniature golden hamster. Dwarf hamsters are a different animal species with their own characteristics and care requirements.

The dwarf hamster, with a weight of scarcely fifty grams, is among the smallest rodents. The adjective "dwarf" says something about its size. The word "hamster" comes from the German word *"hamstern"* which means to "amass" or "pile up." The dwarf hamster does this with the help of small cheek pouches.

External appearance

Dwarf hamsters resemble small mice, but lack the long tail. They are round, with short legs, a small tail, a woolly coat and a head with small ears and rather large, round beady eyes. Like all other rodents, the dwarf hamster is equipped with a set of strong incisors. There are at least fifteen known species of dwarf hamster, ranging from

the Mongolian dwarf hamster to the Tibetan dwarf hamster. Only four of these species are kept as domestic pets:
- the Russian dwarf hamster *(Phodopus sungorus sungorus)*
- Campbell's dwarf hamster *(Phodopus sungorus Campbelli)*
- the Roborovski dwarf hamster *(Phodopus roborovskii)*
- the Chinese dwarf hamster *(Cricetulus griseus)*

The Russian dwarf hamster is often called "Russian" for short and the Chinese dwarf hamster "Chinese." The Roborovski dwarf hamster is also known affectionately as a "Robby." The dwarf hamster species which are kept as domestic pets weigh between thirty and fifty grams and are five to twelve centimeters long. They live for one-and-a-half to four years on average.

In zoos, and the private collections of specialized hamster fanciers, we sometimes come across the mouselike hamster *(Calomyscus bailwardi)*. This species, in fact, resembles a mouse more than a dwarf hamster and has a long tail.

A dwarf hamster weighs about 50 grams, a tame rat nearly ten times as much

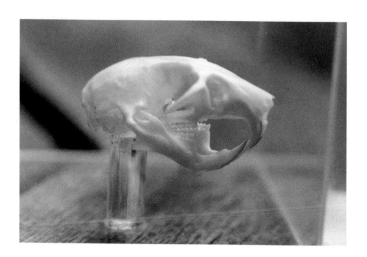

Original habitat

The original habitat of the dwarf hamsters lies in Central
Asia, including China (Northeast China, Manchuria),
Mongolia, Kazakhstan and parts of Russia (Siberia).
Dwarf hamsters live there in relatively wild and dry
areas, principally steppes, sandy plains and prairies and
semi-deserts and, depending on the species, sometimes
in more wooded and mountainous areas. They also feel
at home around nomad settlements and their sheep
flocks and on farmland. The Asian farming population
is not so happy with the dwarf hamster because the creature likes to eat a share of their grain harvest. They,
therefore, often regard the wild congeners of the little
hamsters which we spoil as domestic pets as vermin.
Wild dwarf hamsters usually live in pairs or in family
groups, but there are also species which prefer a solitary
existence and therefore live alone. Dwarf hamsters do
not hibernate. Thanks to their woolly fur coats and hairy
paws, ears and tail, they are able to withstand the cold
quite well. The dwarf hamster's natural enemies are
birds of prey, such as owls, and foxes. These predators
strike mainly at the time when the dwarf hamsters can
no longer escape so quickly because of their bulging
cheek pouches.

The dwarf hamster nest

Wild dwarf hamsters generally live in simple burrow systems under the ground. They are not very good at nest
building. Sometimes they make a shelter under stones or

Deserts are the original home of Roborovski dwarf hamsters

tree roots or they take over, very conveniently, a home made by other rodents. The dwarf hamster nest is situated several tens of centimeters under the ground. The Roborovski generally lives in a round nest chamber at the end of a fifty to one hundred-centimeter long horizontal tube with only one entrance. The Russian dwarf hamster builds a rather more extensive home consisting of a horizontal passage about a meter long, a nest chamber and a number of vertical shafts which are connected to the

Dwarf hamsters like to retreat into their burrows

horizontal passage. When danger threatens, the dwarf hamster can run to the nearest shaft and drop into it in order to bring itself to safety. Dwarf hamsters line their nest chambers with camel hair, sheep's wool or dry grass and construct a store chamber in which a couple of hundred grams up to (sometimes) several kilos of food can be stored for periods of scarcity.

Behavior

Dwarf hamsters are naturally active mainly at night, particularly at dawn and dusk, when they leave their nests to gather food. But the majority of species are also active for short periods during the day. Dwarf hamsters have their own language. They communicate with each other by means of a variety of sounds, ranging from soft, high-pitched squeaks to a very shrill screech. Dwarf hamsters also communicate through their sense of smell. They possess special glands which secrete a scent. Depending upon the species, these glands are situated on the belly or the flanks, but also behind the ears, in the corners of the eyes and on the cheek pouches. Smells play an important role in the perception environment of the dwarf hamster. Researchers who followed the movements of wild dwarf hamsters and marked them with small, brightly-colored flags discovered that the animals laid out complete "dwarf hamster highways" with the aid of scent trails.

Dwarf hamsters spread their scent by means of grooming movements

They spread their scent by means of various polishing movements (e.g. by scratching behind the ears, rubbing their forepaws over their eyes and muzzle and rolling over the ground). In this way, the dwarf hamster sets out a ground plan which can still be closely followed days later by other dwarf hamsters.

Young dwarf hamster

Campbell's dwarf hamster original color

Body language

Dwarf hamsters make their state of mind clear by means of body movements. Rapid rubbing of the head is often an expression of uncertainty. A prolonged spell of cleaning with the tongue and paws, on the other hand, is a sign that the animal feels at ease. The forepaws are used to make warding-off gestures and to fill or empty the cheek pouches. The hind legs are handy for sitting upright to scan the environs. A well-known form of body language is lying on the back. They display this gesture of fear and subjection both to their own kind and to humans.

From steppe to living room

Family group of Russian dwarf hamsters

Although the dwarf hamster originates from Asia, this small steppe dweller has succeeded amazingly well in adapting itself to a life in captivity. As various naturalists have observed, even animals which have been caught in the wild are naturally friendly and can be quickly tamed. They exchange their burrows under the almost endless

steppe with little difficulty for a bed of sawdust and hay in a small rodent cage. Dwarf hamsters were widely used as laboratory animals. Stocks were established in laboratories in Beijing, the former Leningrad and Moscow, as well as in Germany. From there the dwarf hamsters spread to other laboratories throughout the world. The Chinese dwarf hamster is a well-known laboratory animal in the fields of virology, bacteriology and radiation, cancer and diabetes research. Via the laboratories, the Asian dwarf hamsters found their way to the Western European living rooms. The dwarf hamsters came into vogue as domestic pets in the 1960s and '70s. They have enjoyed great popularity especially since the 1980s and '90s. Its droll appearance, its friendly, inquisitive behavior and the ease of caring for it have made the dwarf hamster much loved throughout the world.

Chinese dwarf hamster

Page 17:
Original color
Chinese dwarf
hamster

2 DWARF HAMSTER SPECIES

A word of introduction

Before you acquire a dwarf hamster, it is important to learn something about the different species because the Russian, Campbell's, Robby and Chinese are all somewhat different in appearance, behavior and character. In this chapter, you will be introduced to the four best known dwarf hamster species which are kept as domestic pets. The different dwarf hamster varieties, or the various colors and coat structures, will be described in a separate chapter.

The Russian dwarf hamster

Of all the dwarf hamsters, the Russian dwarf hamster lives by nature in the northernmost regions. The species was already described scientifically in 1770, but it was not until nearly two centuries later that the Russian dwarf hamster became known as a domestic pet. A colony was established in the Max Planck Institute in Germany with animals caught in Siberia. Russian dwarf hamsters from this colony spread later to laboratories and then to living rooms all over the world. The Russian dwarf hamster is

Original color
Russian dwarf
hamster

also known as the Siberian or Dzungarian (a region in the northwest of China is called Dzungaria) dwarf hamster. An English name is the hairy-footed dwarf hamster. The species is also known as the "western form" of the Russian dwarf hamster, while a related species, Campbell's dwarf hamster, is regarded as the "eastern form." But by far the majority of fanciers simply refer to the Russian dwarf hamster. Like the Campbell's dwarf hamster and the Roborovski dwarf hamster, the Russian dwarf hamster *(Phodopus sungorus)* is a member of the genus Phodopus, the group of short-tailed dwarf hamsters. The stumpy tail of these animals is, therefore, very short and almost completely hidden in the coat. This is why many people who shudder at the long bald tail of a mouse are often not afraid of a Russian dwarf hamster. There are different colored Russians, but the original color is the original color. This is characterized by a grey-brown back and a white abdomen. They further have a very characteristic marking; a black-brown stripe, known as the dorsal stripe, runs along the back from the head to the tail. The boundary between the back color and the abdomen color is marked by a black-brown, wavy line. This is known as the triple-arch line. Because of its nearly globular build, short legs and blunt head with a somewhat Roman hooked nose, the Russian dwarf hamster resembles an endearing, small woolly ball. It is very friendly towards humans and allows itself to be picked up. Children, in particular, often succeed in making a very tame cuddly pet of the Russian.

Some remain rather squeaky and less easy to handle. The Russian dwarf hamster is a sociable animal. In the wild, the animals live in small groups. Russians can also be kept very well together as domestic pets. Russian dwarf hamsters often do not live for much longer than two years, although some do live to by three or four years old.

Winter White

During the winter months, the coat of the Russian sometimes turns wholly or partly white under the influence of the decreasing light and of its hormones. In the wild, this makes the animals less conspicuous in the snow. Thanks to this winter coat, the Russian dwarf hamster is called the "Winter White" or "Little winter white" in Great Britain. It is typical of animals in their winter coat that they are temporarily less fertile or infertile.

Russian dwarf hamster in its winter coat

Campbell's dwarf hamster

Campbell's dwarf hamster *(Phodopus Campbelli)* was first described scientifically in 1905. The species is named after its discoverer Campbell, who first encountered this dwarf hamster in Mongolia in 1902. The Campbell is also referred to as the "eastern form" of the Russian dwarf hamster. In Great Britain, where Campbell's dwarf hamster was kept as a domestic pet

than earlier the Russian dwarf hamster, it is known as the "original dwarf hamster" or the Djungarian dwarf hamster. This all adds to the confusion because in other countries it is precisely the Russian that is sometimes referred to as the Djungarian dwarf hamster.

Campbell's is much more temperamental than the Russian dwarf hamster. The character of the latter corresponds most to that of a tame pony, while Campbell's dwarf hamster has more the temperament of a fiery thoroughbred. There are also external differences; Campbell's is more robust in build, its muzzle is rather more pointed and its color in the wild is rather more brownish-yellow. Campbell's dwarf hamster does have

similar markings to the Russian: a dorsal stripe along its back and a triple-arch line over its flanks. Although it may become somewhat lighter and paler in color during the winter, in contrast to the Russian, Campbell's does not acquire a white winter coat.

In the wild, Campbell's dwarf hamster does not live in groups like the Russian dwarf hamster, but in pairs. It is often possible, however, to house more than two Campbell's together in a cage, since they are reasonably tolerant of each other. Campbell's dwarf hamsters often do not live for longer than two years, although some live exceptionally to three or four years.

"Pit-bull hamsters"

Towards people, however, Campbell's dwarf hamsters, particularly the females, can behave rather aggressively. On average, they are not as sweet and docile as Russians. They have even acquired the nickname "Pit-bull hamster" because of their biting habit. This nickname is not undeserved because some Campbell's are so aggressive that they actually jump up in your hands and fix their teeth to your fingertips. This aggressiveness has incidentally been found to be hereditary, and occurs with all colors. Some breeders have succeeded in establishing more friendly Campbell's bloodlines. Animals from these races are generally very easy to handle. Take good note of the character if you want to acquire a Campbell's dwarf hamster. This will help avoid any disappointment associated with coming home with a piranha instead of a cuddly creature.

Campbell's dwarf hamster versus Russian dwarf hamster

Campbell's dwarf hamster greatly resembles the Russian dwarf hamster. The two species are even so closely related that they can be crossed with each other. These crossings can produce fertile offspring which exhibit the characteristics of both the Russian and Campbell's dwarf hamster. Because of the existence of these hybrids, it is sometimes impossible to say whether a dwarf hamster is a Russian or a Campbell's. Many dwarf hamsters are unfortunately no longer purebred. We strongly advise against crossing, partly because it creates fertility problems. Moreover, it results in the loss of the characteristic features of both species.

Russian or Campbell's?
The following are the principal differences between the Russian dwarf
hamster and Campbell's dwarf hamster:

• Russian dwarf hamster	• Campbell's dwarf hamster
globular build, a little ball	more robust and flatter in build
broad, stumpy head	more triangular head
round, Roman nose	more pointed nose
ears small and round	ears somewhat larger
eyes closer to the ears	eyes closer to the nose
bulging beady eyes	eyes a little more deep-set
little eyelid visible	eyelid more visible
original color is grayish brown	original color is brownish-yellow
deeper, darker color	paler, lighter color
more black pigment	more brown pigment
blackish brown triple-arch line	creamy brown triple-arch line
dorsal stripe broader	dorsal stripe thinner
woolly coat	rather smooth coat
grows a winter coat	does not grow a winter coat

The Roborovski dwarf hamster

The third short-tailed hamster is the Roborovski dwarf hamster (*Phodopus roborovskii*). This is the smallest and also the least known dwarf hamster. It was first caught during an expedition in 1894 and was first scientifically described in 1903. In comparison with the other dwarf hamster species, the "Robby," as the species is called by fanciers, is still fairly rare. While the Russian and Campbell's live more on steppes covered with grass and bushesin the wild, the Roborovski dwarf hamster prefers a more sandy terrain to which its color is adapted. The Robby has a pale brownish-yellow to dull sandy-yellow back, with a rusty brown sheen. The bottom of the hairs is blue in color. Because the coat is rather open, this blue color shines somewhat through the yellow. The abdomen is clear white. The Roborovski dwarf hamster has no dorsal stripe and no triple-arch line, so that it cannot be confused with the Russian or Campbell's. The Robby has a conspicuous white spot over each eye. A further characteristic is its large white moustache with strongly developed whiskers. This species has the shortest life of all the dwarf hamsters: one-and-a-half to two years is generally the maximum. Roborovski dwarf hamsters can be kept in pairs or groups. A striking feature is their particularly busy behavior. In the wild they dash at breakneck speed from one hiding place to another, but they also move like lightning as domestic pets. They are often compared with fleas because of their quick jumpy movements. Anyone who enjoys peace will certainly feel more than a little nervous in the presence of a cage full of Robbies skeltering to and from. Because Roborovski dwarf hamsters are so quick and busy, they are difficult to pick up and hard to handle. For children who like to cuddle an animal, the acquisition of a busy bee like the Robby will, therefore, often end in disappointment.

The Roborovski dwarf hamster has a conspicuous white spot over each eye

The Chinese dwarf hamster

In contrast to the Russian, Campbell's and Roborovski dwarf hamsters, the Chinese dwarf hamster *(Cricetulus griseus)* is a member of the genus Cricetulus, the group of long-tailed dwarf hamsters. Instead of the inconspicuous small, hairy, waggly tail of the short-tailed dwarf hamsters, the Chinese has a longer, thinner and more prominent tail, which may reach a length of 2.5 centimeters. Not only is its tail longer, but the body of the Chinese is also longer, slimmer and more scrawny than that of the more cuddly short-tailed species. The species was first described scientifically in 1867 and has bred in captivity at least since 1919. The Chinese dwarf hamster is also known by the names striped hamster and rat-like hamster. The Chinese dwarf hamster has a brownish-grey back and a white abdomen in the wild. Like the Russian and Campbell's, the Chinese has a dark dorsal stripe, but it does not have the triple-arch line. The boundary between the back and abdomen colors in the Chinese dwarf hamster follows a straight line. In the wild, the Chinese feels at home in rather more wooded and mountainous areas. Thanks to its streamlined build, it can climb reasonably well. Its tail serves as a rudder and extra hand, which it can curl to get a better grip around objects. The Chinese lives relatively long by dwarf hamster standards. Ages of up to four years are possible. By nature, the Chinese dwarf hamster is a solitary creature. It therefore does not mind being alone. Sometimes people manage to keep the animals in pairs or even family groups, but Chinese are often very intole-

Left, the long-tailed Chinese; right, the short-tailed Russian

---

Short or long-tailed?
The following are the principal differences between the short-tailed Russian, Campbell's and Roborovski dwarf hamster and the long-tailed Chinese dwarf hamster:

• **Short-tailed dwarf hamster:**	• **Long-tailed dwarf hamster:**
round in build	longer, more stretched in build
chubby	slimmer
short tail (0.5-1 cm)	longer tail (c. 2.5 cm)
triple-arch line along flanks (except Roborovski)	straight line along flanks
quite woolly coat	smoother coat
less nimble	good climber

---

rant of each other, so that fierce fights may arise, in which the animals literally bite each other to pieces and eat each other up like real cannibals. The females are generally the most aggressive. The testicles of the Chinese dwarf hamster are strongly developed. The scrotum sometimes even takes up one-third of the total body length. Not everyone is enamored of this "build." Despite its sometimes bloodthirsty behavior towards its

*Original color
Chinese dwarf
hamster*

own kind, the Chinese are particularly gentle and lovable towards humans. It is less squeaky and liable to bite than the short-tailed dwarf hamsters. Anyone who is not interested in breeding results and is wary of fights, would do well to keep a single Chinese. They will then have a darling or a companion and no risk of fatal bloodbaths.

*Chinese dwarf
hamsters are
reasonably good
climbers*

Campbell's dwarf hamster

The Chinese dwarf hamster does not get on well with its congeners

Which species appeals to you most?

- Russian dwarf hamster: good for keeping in groups
  friendly and readily tamed
  easy to handle
  sometimes rather squeaky
- Campbell's dwarf hamster: usually good for keeping together
  spirited character, sometimes liable to bite
  sometimes less easy to handle
- Roborovski dwarf hamster: good for keeping together
  lightning quick and very busy
  difficult to handle, mainly fun to watch
- Chinese dwarf hamster: aggressive towards its own kind
  lovable and gentle towards humans
  sometimes quick, but easy to handle

Page 29:
Blue, natural-
colored Russian
dwarf hamster

3 CHOOSING AND BUYING A DWARF HAMSTER

Does a dwarf hamster suit you?

After you have chosen the species among the different dwarf hamsters which most appeals to you, you can go looking for your favorite dwarf or dwarves. But, even if you have already decided or if the children are already complaining, always think very carefully before you buy one or more dwarf hamsters. Every animal, even if it is only a very small one, requires daily attention and care. Provided it has sufficient food and water, a dwarf hamster can certainly be left at home alone for a weekend, but if you are leaving home for longer or going on vacation, you will have to find someone who is willing to care for the animal. These are things which you have to take into account. Some dwarf hamsters are suitable for holding in the hand and stroking. Other species, particularly the Roborovski dwarf hamster, prefer just to be looked at. If you like to spend time fondling an animal, you would do better not to choose a dwarf hamster. Only limited cuddling is possible because of its small size. Although the majority of dwarves will climb into their owner's hand for a little attention and a stroke on occasion. Because of their curiosity, they quickly allow themselves to be tamed. Some animals even like to travel on their owner's hand or arm. Above all, dwarf hamsters are very entertaining animals to watch; life is never dull in a dwarf hamster cage.

Russian dwarf hamsters are very curious

*There is always
something
happening in
a dwarf-hamster
cage*

Where to buy?

Where you can best acquire a dwarf hamster depends
very much on the species. You can buy a Russian dwarf
hamster in most pet stores, but Roborovski dwarf hamsters and Chinese dwarf hamsters are mostly obtainable
only from fanciers who breed these species. The color
you bring home will depend not only on your preferen-
ce, but also on the supply. In the pet store, often only
original-colored animals are on sale because this is the
most common color among dwarf hamsters. If you are
looking for a special or rare color, such as a yellow
Campbell's dwarf hamster or a dappled Chinese dwarf
hamster, you will generally have to go to a specialized
breeder of that color. A local or national association of
small rodent fanciers will often be able to help you further. The prices for a dwarf hamster incidentally vary
widely. A private individual sometimes gives them away
free, while a serious breeder may ask a considerable sum
for an animal with a special or new color. Here is a useful tip: during pet shows, fanciers often dispose of their
breeding products for a moderate sum.

Choosing

When you buy a dwarf hamster, always pay careful attention to the age, health and character of the animal. To
begin with, dwarf hamsters should not be too old or too
young. It is better not to buy an animal that is younger

than six weeks or older than about six months. In view of the short lifespan of dwarf hamsters, if you buy an older animal, you will not have much enjoyment from it. Moreover, if they have not yet become accustomed to human hands, older dwarf hamsters are rather more difficult to tame. Animals which are younger than six weeks are usually still too weak to stand on their own legs. In addition, you should always examine carefully the condition of the animals you are offered. The dwarf hamster which you buy must look healthy. This means that the little creature must have a glossy, full coat and its eyes must be clear. Go elsewhere if you encounter animals with dirty eyes, ears, nose or anus. This also applies to injuries, bald patches, scales, scabs or vermin. Never buy a thin animal, as thin dwarf hamsters are either out of condition or are already very old. If all that is in order, then observe the animal's character. Take up the dwarf hamsters which most appeal to you in your hands or allow them to sniff your hands carefully and watch how they react. It is normal for the animals to be somewhat fearful or cautious at first when they see strange fingers. A dwarf hamster will not generally rest in your hands immediately, but you would do well to refuse a truly timid, aggressive and vicious animal or equally one that is listless and apathetic. Lastly, look at the cage in which the animals are housed. It must smell fresh (even from very close by) and be clean. The animals must have sufficient food, fresh drinking water and the cage must not be over-

Yellow, natural-colored Campbell's dwarf hamsters

Roborovski dwarf hamsters

crowded. If too many dwarf hamsters live in too small an area, there is a high likelihood of stress in the cage. And it is precisely the animals subject to stress who are more susceptible to disease.

Male or female?

Because of the woolly coat, it is not always easy to determine the sex of short-tailed-dwarf hamsters. The distance

This little Russian has a clear look in its eyes

between the anus and the genital opening is greater with the males than the females. With young animals in particular, a lot of fumbling is needed to see that properly, and mistakes are sometimes made. With the males, the scent gland on the abdomen is often clearly visible as a yellowish, greasy spot. Sexing is much easier with the long-tailed Chinese dwarf hamster because of the prominent testicles of the males.

Whether you choose a male or a female makes little difference as far as character is concerned. There are few character differences between the two sexes, except for the Chinese dwarf hamster, where the females are often fiercer towards their congeners. The males of the Russian dwarf hamster generally get on better with each other than the males of the Campbell's dwarf hamster. This has to do with the fact that the Russian is accustomed to living in groups, while Campbell's live together in pairs in the wild. The Campbell's male therefore displays more aggression towards other males because he has to defend his female and his territory against intruders. Anyone who places animals of a different sex together will undoubtedly obtain young. Enlarging a family is fun, but with the Russian and Campbell's dwarf hamsters, in particular, the number of births can soon get out of hand. If you do not want nests, it is better to take two or more animals of the same sex.

Before you know it, you will have a mob of young dwarf hamsters

Transport

It is an excellent idea to buy a handy, portable plastic car-rying box at the same time as you buy your dwarf ham-ster, since any dwarf hamster worth its salt quickly manages to gnaw its way through the cardboard box that is usually provided for it. You can transport your new acquisition safely and comfortably in a carrying box. Moreover, the box will later prove useful if the hamster has to be "parked" while its cage is being cleaned or if it has to go on a journey, such as to a show or to the veteri-narian.

Bare necessities

If you buy a dwarf hamster, you will, at least, need the following:

- carrying box
- cage
- floor covering
- nesting material
- toys
- feeding trough
- drinking bottle
- food

How many dwarf hamsters?

Take at least two animals if you choose to buy a short-tailed dwarf hamster like the Russian dwarf hamster because Russian dwarf hamsters are social animals, accustomed by nature to live in groups. They can also be kept in pairs. Campbell's dwarf hamsters live in pairs in the wild, but can often also be housed in groups. Roborovski dwarf hamsters can usually live together either in pairs or in small groups. Because of their vicious behavior towards their fellows, Chinese dwarf hamsters must often be housed alone, although some races are tolerant, so that these Chinese can live in pairs or even groups. Because the females are often the troublemakers, it is better to keep only males of these species together. Several males with one or two females or an older male with a young female are combinations which work better than several females with one or two males or an older female with a young male. One can never say with certainty whether two or more dwarf hamsters will click and continue to click. Some squabbling and angry squeaking goes with establishing the mutual pecking order. Sometimes a bloody war may suddenly break out within a pair or group after a long period of peace and harmony. If the animals are constantly harassing one another, or if they are causing bodily harm to each other, one has no choice but to separate the ringleaders, and to house the dominant animals separately.

Russian dwarf hamster

You always have to wait and see whether they will click

Allow the animals to become habituated to each other

It is best to allow dwarf hamsters to grow up with each other from when they are young. The animals do not necessarily have to come from the same nest, but they must be of about the same size and age (not older than three months). It is, in fact, unwise to place different species of dwarf hamsters together, partly because of their very different lifestyles and characteristics.

There is no fixed recipe for allowing dwarf hamsters to habituate to each other, and allowing older animals to habituate to each other will always be a gamble. Sometimes it goes well, sometimes it will be a territorial life and death struggle. Often peace will be quickly made after a turbulent introduction with the attendant chases and attacks. When introducing new animals you can use one of more of the tricks listed in the box. In any event, never place completely strange animals together, and keep a good watch on dwarf hamsters who have recently been introduced to each other during the first few days. Always ensure that there are sufficient hiding places in the cage, so that the animals have an opportunity to withdraw for a "time-out." Dwarf hamsters who have lived alone for too long, have been temporarily separated from their fellows or have lost their partner can sometimes, unfortunately, no longer be paired with their congeners.

Introduce dwarf hamsters to each other

• The strange territory trick:
introduce the dwarf hamsters to each other outside their territory on neutral ground.

• The clean cage trick:
place the dwarf hamsters in a cage that has been thoroughly cleaned, so that it no longer contains any familiar scents.

• The switching trick:
place the dwarf hamsters in separate cages. Switch the animals' cages after a week, so that they can peacefully accustom themselves to each other's scent.

• The mesh trick:
place the newcomer or newcomer's box inside the cage of the animals already in occupation. The parties can then first become acquainted through the wire mesh.

• The treats trick:
put down food in the cage which is so delicious that the dwarf hamsters forget about each other.

• The perfume trick:
place a tiny (!) drop of perfume or toilet water on the animals' coats, so that they all smell the same.

Spotted Chinese dwarf hamster

4 HANDLING
DWARF HAMSTERS

Becoming acquainted

First allow the dwarf hamster to accustom itself peacefully to its new surroundings for a day or so. Then you can start to become acquainted. Go about it quietly because groping and grasping will frighten the animal. Dwarf hamsters who are not yet used to people will run away in the first instance. They may turn on their backs from fear and in self-defense, emitting a shrill screech.

Start by allowing the dwarf hamster to sniff your hand and allow it to become accustomed to your smell, voice and physical movements. Attract the animal with something tasty (e.g. a sunflower seed or a raisin). Curiosity will generally quickly get the better of fear. Through daily attention, the dwarf hamster will gradually grow used to your presence. You can determine for yourself how tame you want to make your new domestic pets. It is, in any event, convenient if the animal is sufficiently manageable to allow you to pick it up to examine its teeth or claws, for example.

Biting?

If an otherwise tame dwarf hamster uses its teeth, it usually has a good reason. The animal may have been frightened of something, woken up roughly or unexpectedly or perhaps your fingers smell of food, unfamiliar scents or other animals. But it may also be that something is wrong with its surroundings, its care or the animal itself.

Tempting with a tasty morsel

Picking up

A dwarf hamster should always be picked up and held very carefully. Dwarf hamsters are small and very vulnerable animals; pinching them hard can cause irreparable internal injury. Moreover, the young animals, especially, are impetuous and can make unexpected leaps. In the wild, dwarf hamsters who feel threatened let themselves drop into a vertical shaft. Dwarf hamsters kept as domestic pets may use the same trick if they see "bird of prey-like" hands gliding overhead. Because dwarf hamsters cannot see very well and have little sense of depth, they often do not hesitate in such a situation to jump down from a table. And such an unexpected jump may be fatal. The best approach is to pick up the dwarf hamster carefully by creating a kind of bowl with your two hands. Allow it to sit in one hand, while holding the other hand over the animal like a protective roof. Very fearful and jumpy animals can best be "shoveled up" into a container. The center of a toilet roll can be very handy for picking up a rather nervous or vicious dwarf hamster. The animal usually runs into the roll of its own accord. It is also possible to persuade the dwarf hamster to walk onto a piece of wire netting. The netting gives the animal something to hold onto and some security. It is sometimes necessary to hold a dwarf hamster really securely, which is known as "fixing." You can do this by holding

They must be picked up very carefully

the animal securely by the nape of the neck with two fingers. Most dwarf hamsters do not like being held in this
way, but fixing is sometimes necessary in order to sex or
examine a dwarf hamster.

Escaped!

Dwarf hamsters cannot be let out of their cage. The danger is too great that someone will tread on them, that
they will be caught by other domestic pets such as a dog,
cat or ferret, or will run away during a reconnoitering
expedition and be lost forever. Moreover, dwarf hamsters
may start gnawing at electric wiring, your brand new
floor covering or the precious antique cabinet. Once they
have reached the ground, they are lightning quick and
almost impossible to catch. In brief, an escaped dwarf
hamster (and they do sometimes escape!) is no picnic.
Tough as they are, escaped dwarf hamsters can survive
for a long time. There is little sense in chasing an escaped dwarf hamster. You would do better to take advantage of its curiosity. Try, for example, to tempt it to walk
into a box placed on its side containing food. Placing the
dwarf hamster cage on the ground with the door open
may also work. It is very likely that once the dwarf hamster has calmed down, it will return to its cage to eat or
sleep. You can try setting a trap by putting down a small

tray or small bowl containing some nesting material and tempting food. Build some steps, for example, from books or small blocks of wood stacked against the tray. Attracted by the food, the dwarf hamster often allows itself to fall into the tray from the steps and then cannot get out. It may be possible to put down a large mousetrap of the type in which the animal can be caught alive (!). Peanut butter is an ideal bait for this. It may happen that you do not precisely know in which part of the house the escaped dwarf hamster is hiding. In that case, you can put down a known number of sunflower seeds in each room. If seeds have disappeared somewhere the next day, you will know where the dwarf hamster has been.

Before you know it, he has gone...

Dwarf hamsters and children

Children often have the dwarf hamster high on their list of favorite animals. Dwarf hamsters are, however, certainly not toys and are not able to tolerate pinching and grasping from a child's hands. Parents must teach their children that a dwarf hamster is a vulnerable creature that needs a lot of rest. You cannot leave the care of

Roborovski dwarf hamsters

Dwarf hamsters are not toys

a dwarf hamster to your children; one of the adult family members must always take on this task. One can think up all kinds of amusing things to engage children actively with their dwarf hamster. They can, for example, make a little sleeping house from a cardboard box or flower pot, build a climbing frame from empty toilet rolls or put together a real dwarf hamster maze with pieces of pvc tubing. And the dwarf hamster is, of course, a very suitable subject for a school talk or project. The dwarf hamster has a rather short life. On the one hand, this may be seen as an advantage: the dwarf hamster is not an animal with which you are stuck for ten years or more, but on the other hand, you must take into account that your children will be confronted through the dwarf hamster with the unavoidable concept of death. The death of a dwarf hamster does give you the opportunity to explain this concept. The loss of a domestic pet can be very traumatic for children, but the grief can usually be borne better if it is worked through in the right manner. You can let the children write a poem about, or a letter to, the dwarf hamster, for example, in order to ease the grief, and then bury the animal together.

Claws

Dwarf hamsters are very easy animals to care for. The daily care of the dwarf hamster consists mainly of giving

The claws of this Campbell's are too long

it food and attention. During the weekly cleaning of the cage you can submit it to a minor "overhaul." Check its overall condition and, particularly, the claws and the teeth. Excessively long claws are very common, especially among somewhat older dwarf hamsters. Sometimes the claws even curl right round, so that the animal has difficulty in walking. The points of the claws can then be carefully clipped with a small pair of scissors. If you do this yourself, take care that you do not cut into the sensitive blood vessel that runs through the claw like a red thread. This is a delicate task and not everyone feels able to do it themselves. If you are hesitant to cut the claws yourself, it is better to leave it to a veterinarian. In any event, do not let the animal run around with long claws, as this is very painful and not fair to the animal that is dependent on you for its care.

Teeth

By grasping your dwarf hamster by the nape of the neck, you can examine its teeth. If the front incisors are not properly aligned with each other, they go on growing until they project out of the mouth or become jammed in the oral cavity. We call this phenomenon elephant teeth. Animals with dental problems often salivate and slowly

Russian dwarf hamsters

lose weight because they can no longer eat properly. If your hamster's teeth are not properly aligned with each other and go on growing, call in the veterinarian immediately. He or she can shorten the teeth. This has to be done repeatedly if the teeth grow too long. Anyone who is very handy can learn to cut the teeth to the right length themselves with a small pair of pliers; this spares the animal the stress of a visit to the veterinarian. Yellow or orange teeth among dwarf hamsters are incidentally quite normal. Broken teeth will grow again spontaneously, but it is advisable to check whether the tooth concerned is not starting to grow crookedly.

The abdominal gland

It is a good habit to check the abdominal gland of short-tailed dwarf hamsters regularly. This is a gland on the middle of the abdomen, which is particularly conspicuous with males as a greasy, somewhat yellowish spot. This gland may get dirty and become infected, after which it is covered by a yellowish-brown scab. The skin around the abdominal gland may then turn red and swell up. Try to clean the gland carefully with lukewarm water. If the condition does not then clear up, it is better to consult a veterinarian.

Fixing a dwarf hamster – this animal has a dirty abdominal gland

Coat care

Dwarf hamsters are clean animals and groom their fur nicely themselves. Coat care is therefore seldom necessary. Some animals, particularly the Roborovski dwarf hamsters, which originate from sandy regions, greatly appreciate a sand bath. For this purpose, you can place a small bowl of chinchilla sand in the cage. This sand can be bought in any good pet store. Bathing in the fine sand keeps the coat in good condition. Well-groomed dwarf hamsters are little troubled by such vermin as fleas, lice, mites and molds. Alarm signals which may point to the presence of these parasites include itching, scratching, bald patches, small wounds, scabs or a red, irritated skin. Mites and lice can be successfully controlled with a spray that is suitable for birds. Do not forget to spray the cage as well. Remember that dwarf hamsters are small and delicate animals— never use an anti-flea spray that is intended for cats and dogs. For all parasites, use a safe and preferably natural pesticide that is suitable for dwarf

This by no means always succeeds!

hamsters, if necessary, in consultation with the veterinarian.

Dwarf hamsters and other domestic pets

Dwarf hamsters and other domestic pets do not go well together. Some dogs will sometimes tolerate dwarf hamsters in their vicinity, but the size difference is much too great to really allow them to go around with each other. Cats and ferrets regard dwarf hamsters chiefly as little mice to be stalked and caught. One should also keep a good lookout for other rodents. If dwarf hamsters come into contact with tame rats or golden hamsters (Syrian hamsters), their death warrant is nearly always signed. Because some domestic pets are very astute or strong, it is better not to place a dwarf hamster's cage in a place where a domestic pet such as a tame rat, ferret, cat or dog often hangs around without your supervision.

Dwarf hamsters do not go well with other rodents

5 THE CAGE

Living space

It is often said and written that a small hamster needs only a small box in which to live, but that is certainly a misconception. Unfortunately, many dwarf hamsters, nevertheless, live in a portable plastic container that is really intended only for transport or for very temporary accommodation. Such accommodation is much too confined. Allow for a space of at least 50 x 40 x 30 centimeters for a pair or small group of dwarf hamsters. The more generous the accommodation, the better it is for the animals. It must be at least "dwarf hamsterproof." When buying the cage, ensure that it is specifically suitable for dwarf hamsters, since the bars of many rodent cages often present escape opportunities for dwarf hamsters. Another disadvantage of a cage with bars is that the dwarf hamster may spill a lot of sawdust during its burrowing activities, leaving you to clear up a mess around the cage with some regularity. A large glass or plastic (aquarium) tank provides more satisfactory housing. A cover of wire netting on the tank will keep intruders such as cats out of the tank and the dwarf hamsters—especially jumpers like the Roborovski dwarf hamsters—in. There are all kinds of colorful rodent housing on the market, complete with tube systems, lookout towers, bedrooms and fitness rooms. But these, often expensive structures, may have disadvantages. They are

Example of a glass tank fitted out for dwarf hamsters

often difficult to clean, rapidly fall apart, are poorly ventilated and provide relatively little floor space.

Fitting out and location

You will be doing your dwarf hamster a great favor by providing it with a large "bare" tank, which you can then fit out according to your own taste. In the pet store, you will find all kinds of accessories for fitting out the dwarf hamster tank, from little sleeping houses to sets of steps. When you buy these accessories always ensure that your dwarf hamster cannot get caught or fall out from somewhere because a dwarf hamster requires only a small hole or slit in which to get caught or from which to escape. All dwarf hamsters like a peaceful, dark niche into which they can withdraw. You can buy different models of rodent houses in the pet store, but a small wooden bird nest box also makes a suitable hiding place, as does a decorative terra-cotta flowerpot. The dwarf hamster tank should incidentally not be placed near a draft or in the full sun. Dwarf hamsters thrive best at a temperature of between 59 and 70 °F. The humidity should preferably be between 40 and 60 %. If you set up a decorative tank containing a group of dwarf hamsters in a prominent position in the living room, possibly with lighting from above, you will have your own "dwarf hamster television," which is often much more interesting to watch than the TV.

Running wheel

Many readymade dwarf hamster tanks are equipped with a running wheel as a standard item. Such a wheel has its advantages and disadvantages. It is good for the animal's physical condition, but on the other hand, "jogging" on such a wheel often becomes compulsive. If your dwarf hamster also runs for hours on end in its running

Steps for climbing

Campbell's dwarf hamsters housed on beech chippings

With a running wheel with bars you have to take care that the animals do not get trapped between the bars

wheel, don't allow the wheel to stay permanently in the tank so that the animal exhausts itself. If you want to acquire a running wheel for your dwarf hamsters, it is best to buy a closed one because with a wheel with bars you run the risk that the dwarf hamster will become caught, especially if several animals use the wheel at the same time. Dwarf hamsters can cover a good distance. In the wild they are very mobile and regularly venture a couple of hundred meters from their nest to look for food. A diligent father who connected the running wheel of his daughter's dwarf hamster to a bicycle computer, re-

corded distances from 2.5 to no less than 5.5 miles per day! The dwarf hamster ran from two to nearly five hours daily in the wheel and achieved an average speed of 1.1 to over 1.2 miles per hour.

Floor cover and nest material

A good layer sawdust or coarse shavings, also known as wood fiber, is very suitable as a floor covering. Dwarf hamsters enjoy digging down and scurrying about in a "sawdust bath." There are other kinds of floor covers for small rodents on the market such as pellets and small wood blocks, which are very absorbent, almost dust-free and, moreover, can be made into compost. Dwarf hamsters can generally, however, not dig so readily in these materials. Avoid products with a strong pine or menthol aroma, which can cause allergies. Many dwarf hamsters appreciate a dish of fine (chinchilla) sand in which they can look after their coats. Dwarf hamsters build a comfortable bedroom from a sizable bunch of aromatic hay. Shreds of paper and strips of kitchen roll are also suitable for making a nice nest. In any event, always ensure there is enough nest material. The special "bedding" of cotton or synthetic material which is on the market has certain dangerous disadvantages and so is unsuitable for dwarf hamsters. The animals may swallow this white, fluffy product or become trapped in it, so that they choke, or suffer constipation or pinched limbs as a result.

Head down in a sawdust bath

Cleaning

Dwarf hamsters do not smell and their droppings are hard, dry and odorless. Cleaning the tank once a week is, therefore, generally more than enough. When you do so, replace the floor covering and the nest material and wash out the tank, if necessary, with hot water and a mild detergent. Also regularly clean the fittings of the tank. Most hamsters reserve one corner of their tank for urinating. If you wish, you can clean this toilet corner somewhat more often. Ensure that the quarters, certainly if they are a plastic or glass tank in which less ventilation is possible, are always clean and dry. This will prevent the chance of condensation and the persistence of harmful ammonia fumes from the urine.

A dwarf hamster jungle

The life of dwarf hamsters can be made considerably more enjoyable by giving them exciting quarters, in which they can indulge their natural behavior to the fullest. If the animals are invited to explore, to climb and to run, that has yet another advantage, which is that they do not grow too fat and so will lead a longer and healthier life. You can fit out a complete dwarf hamster jungle according to your own taste, which approaches the natural habitat as closely as possible. The Roborovski dwarf hamster lives naturally in sandy regions. You will give it a lot of pleasure by providing it with its own private desert consisting of a layer of sand and a few stones. For the Russian and Campbell's dwarf hamster you can try to imitate a steppe with grass, sand and stones. As a climber,

Cleaning the quarters once a week is generally more than enough

the Chinese dwarf hamster, which comes from more forested and mountainous regions, can be made happy with stones to climb on or branches to climb in.

Behavior enrichment

Cardboard boxes, paper pellets, climbing frames of wire netting and toilet rolls are very suitable materials for what is attractively called "cage enrichment" and leads, using an equally attractive term, to "behavior enrichment." In other words, they enable the dwarf hamster to do that for which it was made: digging, gnawing, climbing and exploring. Regularly offer your dwarf hamster new play materials. Because the animals need not worry about avoiding enemies and finding food, our dwarf hamsters, in contrast to their wild opposite numbers, who are fully engaged in surviving, have oceans of time. It is your task to ensure that there is also something to occupy them in that "free time"!

Proper materials for natural and decorative furnishing of the dwarf hamster's box:

Branches (not poisonous e.g. willow or fruit trees), bamboo tree stumps, dry leaves, brick, bits of floor tile, pebbles, gravel, pieces of wood, sand (dry and not sharp), hay, straw, climbing ropes, terra-cotta flower pots, earthenware bowls, wicker baskets, shells, burlap, raw sheep's wool, corncobs, grass stalks, coconuts, spruce cones.

Stereotypical behavior

Some dwarf hamsters exhibit stereotypical behavior, which means that they endlessly repeat certain movements. They continually dig in the same corner, run to and from along the glass for hours on end or continuously jump up and down in the same spot in an attempt to reach the top. It is the kind of behavior that you also encounter in zoos, the best known example being the pacing up and down of the polar bear.

A Swiss psychologist at the University of Zurich has done research into stereotypical digging movements among Mongolian gerbils. He discovered that these rodent's compulsive digging had nothing to do with the size of their quarters (because whatever their size, the gerbils continued to dig), but was related to the fitting out of those quarters. In the wild, gerbils dig in order to construct underground passage systems. The Swiss researcher, therefore, decided to lay out the gerbils' quarters in such a way that the building of such a passage system became possible. He found that the animals who subsequently grew up in the passage system no longer exhibited stereotypical digging. There was no reason for them

Chinese dwarf hamster busy rope climbing

Roborovski dwarf hamster, note the strikingly well-developed whiskers

Campbell's dwarf hamster, black-eyed white

to dig because a passage system was already there. This knowledge may also prove useful in the housing of dwarf hamsters. If we know why they exhibit certain behavior, we can try to fit out their quarters to accommodate it. What if a dwarf hamster runs endlessly back and forth between the walls of his tank in an attempt to collect food? If that is so, it might help to scatter the food around the tank, so that the creature has to go and search for it and collect it himself. It would be nice if compulsive behavior could be cured by a little thought and experimentation.

Page 61:
This Russian
dwarf hamster is
a little on the
plump side

6 FOOD AND DRINK

Seeds and bugs

In the wild, dwarf hamsters eat mainly the seeds of plants and shrubs. Not everyone will know that, besides vegetable food, the menu also includes small invertebrates such as insects (principally beetles), spiders and slugs. The Chinese dwarf hamster even eats a relatively large amount of animal food. The Roborovski dwarf hamster, on the other hand, restricts itself mainly to seeds of herbs and grasses. Dwarf hamsters are fairly unfussy eaters. In the wild, they eat what the local flora provides. Analysis of the contents of cheek pouches and stomachs of trapped animals has shown that the dwarf hamsters are fond of dozens of different plants. The menu of the animals living in the wild includes desert madwort, Siberian peashrub, dragonhead, wild liquorice, sedge, hemp nettle, tormentil and niter bush. They eat mainly the seeds of these plants. They eat little, if anything, of the other parts of plants, such as the leaves, flowers or stems. Observations of naturalists have shown that some dwarf hamsters collect undigested seeds from

Dwarf hamsters are not fussy eaters

cow manure. They walk into a cowpat, so to speak, in order to recover the undigested seeds.

How much?

It is difficult to indicate in grams precisely how much food dwarf hamsters eat in a day because not everything that the animals take out of their bowl is consumed immediately; some of it is carried in the cheek pouches to store places in the cage. Dwarf hamsters eat a relatively large amount in comparison with the somewhat larger rodents, as small animals have a relatively large body surface, so that they lose more body heat and cool off more rapidly. They, therefore, require more fuel than larger animals to maintain their body temperature. But, nevertheless, they remain very small animals and it is found in practice that they are often given too much to eat. In order to prevent the animals from becoming too fat, it is a good idea to wait until the feeding bowl is nearly empty before refilling it. In this way, your dwarf hamster will not get the opportunity to pick only the tasty (calorie-rich) items from its food and you will know *Serve the food in* for certain that it is not lacking anything. Provide the food *a strong, glazed* in a strong, glazed earthenware bowl. These bowls are *earthenware bowl* strong, resistant to gnawing and also easy to keep clean.

The basic menu

Mixed rodent food or "hamster mix" forms the basic menu for the dwarf hamster. It contains ingredients such as wheat, oats, maize, sunflower seeds, pieces of St. John's bread (pods of the carob tree), peanuts, peas and grass pellets.

There are now also specially developed feeds for dwarf hamsters on the market. These have been devised to take into account all the wishes of the little creature, such as more small seeds and animal food in the form of dried insects or shrimp.

Dwarf hamsters do not greatly care for the pressed grass pellets in the mixed rodent food. Rabbit food contains many of these grass pellets and is therefore not suitable for dwarf hamsters. The orange and green pellets which are found in many mixtures are often no more than pieces of dried bread treated with a dye, which is intended to make the product more attractive to the consumer. The animals generally do not enjoy eating it so much. You would do best to look for a rodent feed that contains as few grass pellets as possible and no synthetic colors. The feed must further contain as little dust and grit as possible and should not smell musty or be damp. Because dwarf hamsters in the wild like to eat small seeds, you

Gnawing on a hazelnut

Some occasional
dog or cat pellets
will provide
sufficient animal
proteins

can mix some birdseed or weed seeds through the standard rodent food. In order to ensure that the dwarf hamster eats sufficient animal protein, the menu may be further supplemented with some dog or cat pellets, universal bird food (with dried insects) or a mealworm.

"Greens"

You can supplement your dwarf hamster's meal with "greens." However, take into account that greens contain a great deal of moisture, and that by nature a dwarf hamster's digestive system is not designed for a moisture-rich menu. In order to prevent problems with the digestive system such as diarrhea, don't give it too many greens, or too much fruit. If you want to feed it greens, limit this to slices of carrot, endive leaves, and pieces of apple, for example. They also really like dandelion leaves. It is a question of trying out what your dwarf hamster likes the best. One might like grapes, while another likes cucumber or banana. Some types of cabbage and citrus fruit are less suitable for dwarf hamsters, than are lettuce leaves that bruise easily, and therefore spoil quickly. Only give your pet clean (washed) greens, and always take away any leftovers of fresh products to prevent them from going bad.

Extras

Now and then you can spoil your dwarf hamster with a little extra. Foxtail millet, crusts of bread and cheese, crackers, small pieces of boiled potato or egg, biscuit crumbs, a teaspoonful of soft curd cheese or yogurt, cornflakes, muesli and raisins are all suitable snacks. Nuts, dog biscuits and crackers can also be nibbled and bitten into small pieces. In the specialty pet stores, there are all sorts of special snacks for sale, from bunches of herbs and waffles, to sticks to sharpen their teeth on, to yogurt drops, that your pet will sometimes find very appe-

Feed greenstuff and fruit in moderation

Dwarf hamsters love small seeds, such as Italian millet

tizing, and at other times leave alone. Because dwarf hamsters use their cheek pouches to store their food, you must be careful when giving them sticky substances and sharp shoots or seeds, such as sharp-pointed oats. These can damage and infect the mucous membrane in the cheeks. One thing counts for all little extras – give them in moderation. Your dwarf hamster is only a very small animal, with a very small stomach, so you can easily give it too much too quickly.

Mineral chews

Experience has shown that dwarf hamsters very often do not use the supplied mineral licks to lick or to gnaw. Preparations such as vitamin drops are not necessary as long as the hamster's condition remains good and its food is varied.

Taboo

Snacks for human beings, such as cookies, crisps, sweets and chocolate, are strictly taboo for dwarf hamsters. Also onions, garlic, uncooked beans, raw potatoes (including the leaves and the shoots), the green parts of carrots and tomatoes, sour pickles and rhubarb are not suitable for dwarf hamsters. Also be careful what leaves or twigs you pick from nature. Buttercups, conifers, oak leaves, poppies, hedge bindweed, laburnum, privet, foxgloves, rhododendrons and bulbous plants such as tulips, narcissi, hyacinths and crocuses, are poisonous and can be fatal to your pet.

Drinking water

Dwarf hamsters, even though they originally come from dry areas, must always have fresh drinking water available. A bowl of water is very clumsy, and is quickly contaminated by sawdust, feces, or leftover food. So you can best give your dwarf hamster a practical drinking bottle with a spout, which can be hung on the outside or the inside of its quarters. Refresh the water on a regular basis, and make sure that the bottle stays clean and free of any green algae. Now and then, check that the spout on the bottle is working properly, and that it has not become blocked with remnants of lime. The water must be easily reachable by young, old, and sick or feeble animals. For young dwarf hamsters that are still too small to reach the drinking water bottle, a saucer or bowl of water can be put in their quarters temporarily. Make absolutely sure that there is not too much water because the very small young ones can drown in it. You can always make the

Fresh drinking water is necessary

water less deep by putting some marbles in it. The small dwarf hamsters can then get their moisture by licking the marbles, without any danger of drowning.

Suitable meals

Russian and Campbell's dwarf hamsters, especially, will at some time suffer from being overweight, which is recognizable by pink, thinly haired cushions of fat between the forepaws, and on the belly. If a dwarf hamster gets too fat, it needs a suitable diet. You must then take fat and calorie-rich peanuts, nuts, and sunflower seeds off the menu. Dwarf hamsters with diarrhea must be temporarily switched to a diet without fat and greenstuffs. In the case of intestinal disorders, you can replace parts of the meals with small amounts of rice crackers, cooked rice, zwieback, crusty bread, and hay. A teaspoon of lukewarm chamomile tea, or weak tea without sugar, can help to calm down an unsettled digestion. Short-tailed dwarf hamsters in good condition should feel like sturdy balls. The long-tailed ones are slender, but sturdy. A dwarf hamster is too thin if you can easily feel its ribcage between your thumb *Bon appetit!* and forefinger. If your hamster is too thin, then a really

good pick-me-up is a stew made from a piece of boiled potato, some garden peas, a piece of meat (for example a small piece of boiled chicken), and a few drops of gravy, especially during the cold winter months. Convalescing and growing dwarf hamsters love to lap up a thick mush of rice flour or oat flakes, diluted with milk or water, with a smidgen of grape sugar, and a drop of vitamin C syrup.

Waiting to see what will come out of the pot

Playing with food

Eating a ready-to-eat meal from a small bowl doesn't demand much effort and intelligence from a dwarf hamster. But you can put your hamster to work by hiding its food, or scattering it across its cage, so that it has to find it and collect it itself. As another example, you can treat your pet to a big lump of dry dog food, with which it can be happy for a considerable time. It is also possible to hang some peanuts that you have bought on a string, or a dog biscuit, in its quarters, so the animal has to really exert itself to be able to reach them. Or you can let your hamster open its own nuts. Picking out the grains from ears of wheat is also a good pastime. For a small group of dwarf hamsters, you can fill a pinecone with peanut butter, seeds, and honey, or fill up a hanging bird food net with nice tidbits in it. This gives the animals something to do, and also gives you something nice to watch.

7 FIRST AID AND ILLNESSES

Accidents

For a small rodent like the dwarf hamster, an accident can easily happen. A fall from the table, a fight with another of its kind, or even too tight a cuddle – before you know it, you have a hamster with a light shock, a bad wound, or a broken paw. So it's handy if you know how to give some first aid, in the case of accidents.

Sometimes first aid is not enough. In the case of a serious injury, such as internal damage caused by someone stepping on it, of course, you must immediately take your dwarf hamster to the veterinarian. If you have any doubts,

---

The top ten greatest dangers for dwarf hamsters

1. Falling off a table
2. Children squeezing them too hard with their hands
3. Strong sunlight (overheating)
4. Being attacked by others
5. Being trodden on
6. Other pets
7. Unsafe cage (escaping)
8. Electricity (chewing through the cables)
9. Furniture (getting jammed)
10. Houseplants poisonous to their kind

An alert dwarf hamster

Some plants may be poisonous

the golden rule is: don't try to treat it yourself, but consult an animal clinic. Also, always make sure that a wounded or sick hamster can easily get to its food and drink.

Dwarf hamsters and the veterinarian
Although dwarf hamsters are among the most popular of pets, we seldom see them at the veterinarian. There is a good reason for this. Unfortunately, dwarf hamsters are creatures on which it is especially difficult to operate. Operating is often not possible because they are so small.

This Russian dwarf hamster makes a healthy impression

It is often not worth the while either because of the costs that can be incurred from an operation, combined with the fact that a dwarf hamster has a relatively short lifespan. The prognosis is often not good either – a veterinarian can weigh up whether or not to operate on the animal, but often the chances of survival are slim. If the veterinarian gives you some medicine to take away with you, always make sure that you ask about the correct dosage. Dosing such a very small animal is extremely precise work. It is also not a good idea to try treating it yourself because some medicines are unsuitable, or too strong, for dwarf hamsters.

Bite wounds

Sometimes squabbles or fights between dwarf hamsters can have an unhappy result. In the worst case, this can be a fatality, but usually the loser comes out with a couple of substantial bite wounds. If you have a hamster that is knocked about by the other ones, it is best to keep it separate from them. Most bite wounds, even if at first sight they appear to be rather nasty, generally heal by themselves reasonably quickly. If necessary, you can treat such wounds yourself, with a healing and disinfecting ointment. In this case, remove any sawdust from its cage, and replace it temporarily with compressed granules or blocks of wood. Sawdust will stick to a wound with ointment on it, and there is an extra danger of infection.

Chinese dwarf hamsters, original color and spotted

Breaks

Because of a fall, or when trying to escape from the too tight grip of small hands, a dwarf hamster can end up with a broken leg. Unfortunately, there is not much you can do about this. It will usually cure itself with a lot of rest, although a lump or a kink may remain visible afterwards. A lot worse than a broken paw is a broken spine. A dwarf hamster with a spine or neck injury holds its head to one side, or drags its back legs. Unfortunately, there is not much that can be done about the symptoms of paralysis. In this case, it is better for the animal to have it put to sleep by your veterinarian. This is why you should prevent a fall as much as possible, by telling children that it is best not to pick up their pet, or only under supervision, and then only a short distance from the ground.

Shock

A dwarf hamster can fall into dangerous, and even fatal, shock because of a sudden shortage of circulating blood in its body. Such a shortage cannot only be caused by loss of blood, or dehydration, but also by enormous fear and pain. In the case of tremendous fear, the blood vessels widen, whereby a relative shortage of blood develops in the rodent's body. Very often a fall, fight, overheating (from staying in the sun too long), or a stressful meeting with other household animals (dog, cat or ferret), can lead to shock. Symptoms of being in shock are dizziness, staring eyes, a rapid and irregular heartbeat, and rapid breathing.

Sufficient nest material keeps a dwarf hamster warm

Because, during this state of shock, the blood flows to the most important organs such as the heart, the hamster's paws feel cold. In a state of shock, the mucous membranes in the mouth are pale. Take the suffering animal quickly to a warm, dark, and peaceful place. With rest, warmth, and a strength-giving drink (water with sugar dissolved in it), most dwarf hamsters come to their senses again.

Overheating

When in their natural surroundings, dwarf hamsters, when it gets too hot, crawl into a cool hole in the ground. Because these animals have a thick coat, they cannot stand heat very well – a few minutes in the hot sun can be fatal for a dwarf hamster. In warm weather, never take dwarf hamsters with you on a journey – plastic boxes for transportation can quickly turn into deadly little glasshouses. The characteristics of sunstroke are apathy, feeling limp, unconsciousness, a weak and speeded up pulse, puffing, dribbling, and trembling paws. Take an overheating hamster immediately to a cool, peaceful and dark area. Cool it down with a damp towel, or carefully dab it with (not too cold) water. If the animal can be saved, it will recover in a reasonably short time. Make sure that it has some water available, to prevent dehydration.

Supercooling

If dwarf hamsters are kept in too cold quarters, or in the case that young ones fall out of the nest (this often happens with cages with bars rather than mesh), they can easily become super cooled. Drowsiness and lethargy, slow movements, half-closed eyes, and a staring coat are some of the symptoms of super cooling. The trick here is not to warm the animal up too quickly. It is better to raise its temperature slowly, in your hands, or on a warm waterbed, for example, made from a well-sealed plastic bag filled with lukewarm water, which you wrap in a washcloth. Give the animal a little sugar water to drink, and make sure there is enough warm nesting material available.

Pick-me-ups

After a big shock, dehydration and cold, or in the case of recuperation after an illness, your dwarf hamster will need a pick-me-up. You can make such a drink yourself. Dwarf hamster breeders use various recipes for such a drink. One

example is a special nip for super-cooled animals, consisting of a small drop of brandy or eggnog, with some warm sugar water (water with sugar dissolved in it). In the case of a cold, a lukewarm drink made from one part water, one part milk, and a teaspoon of honey is very effective. Lukewarm water with grape sugar in it also works very well. A good remedy for dehydration is ORS (Oral Rehydration Salts), available from your pharmacy. You can also make this yourself. The basic recipe: eight teaspoons of sugar and one teaspoon of salt, dissolved in one liter of water.

Illnesses

Dwarf hamsters are generally healthy and strong creatures. But there are some disorders to which they are

---

Quarantine

To prevent other animals being affected, it is a good idea to immediately isolate a hamster that appears to be ill, from any other you may have. You can then try to promote the healing process with warmth (70–77 °F), rest, good hygiene, and a suitable meal. If you have any doubts, or if the affliction perseveres, take your hamster to the veterinarian.

General symptoms of illness

Lethargy, slow movements, arched back, creeping away and hiding, sitting huddled up, lack of appetite, weight loss, staring fur, irregular or wheezy breathing, shivering, wet places under the tail or the belly, dirty corners of the mouth, watery nose, swollen eyelids, eyelids sticking together, or watery eyes.

Too little living space can cause stress

susceptible. Sometimes the dwarf hamster's living environment can be the cause of diseases. Breathing problems, allergic reactions, or inflammation of the eyes, for example, can be the result of the bedding material being too dusty, too thin, too sharp, or smelling too strongly (pine or menthol, for example). A dirty environment is often the cause of a swollen gland on the belly. Dwarf hamsters that are exposed to stress (too little rest, being picked up too often, fights with others of their kind, too many animals in one cage), are more susceptible to illnesses. People who know their hamsters a little, quickly spot when the animals are not feeling themselves. This is also often given away by the air in their quarters — somewhat sweet and sickly in the case of diarrhea, for example.

This Russian is not very well, note the drawn-up back and watery eyes

Tumors

Tumors are one of the most well-known causes of dwarf hamster mortality. The Russian and the Campbell's dwarf hamsters are especially very susceptible to swellings. Unfortunately, nothing can be done about this. Usually the dwarf hamster does not suffer much from the swellings, until the moment comes when the swelling becomes too big and really begins to hinder the animal. It is then advisable to have the animal put to sleep. Incidentally, the bulges under the tails of male Chinese dwarf hamsters are sometimes thought to be tumors, but in fact they are its testicles. Full cheek pouches are also sometimes mistaken for swellings.

Diabetes

With Campbell's dwarf hamsters, diabetes frequently occurs. This affliction appears mostly when the animal is a few months old, and is recognizable by a slow loss of weight (in spite of a healthy appetitive), extreme thirst, whereby the drinking bottle is virtually emptied every day, and very frequent urination. Dwarf hamsters with diabetes can get moistness in their bellies, and become blind. Unfortunately, there is little that can be done about the illness itself. Sometimes the animals stay alive for a few more months, after which they finally fall into a coma, or die very suddenly. To prevent dehydration, a special salt solution can be

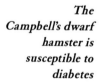

The Campbell's dwarf hamster is susceptible to diabetes

added to the drinking water. It is also sensible to put a hamster with diabetes on a diet that contains the least possible sugars. For this you should check the food packaging, and not only look out for words such as "sugar" and "carbohydrates," but also words like "syrup" and "molasses." Fresh fruit should be avoided for diabetes patients, on account of the fruit sugars that it contains. With dwarf hamsters, diabetes appears to be hereditary, and sometimes entire families (stocks) can be affected. So it is not adviseable to continue breeding animals with diabetes, or their immediate family members. Diabetes in dwarf hamsters can be established by testing the urine, for which a so-called "glucostrip" is used, which is available on the market for human beings with diabetes.

Eye problems

Eye problems, such as cataracts and glaucoma (whereby the eyeball becomes murky or swells up), especially occur with the Campbell's dwarf hamster. Chinese dwarf ham-

Curious

sters sometimes suffer from watery eyes and irritated, open sores around the edges of the eyes. It is best not to treat these yourself, but get a veterinarian in.

Deficiency illnesses

Deficiency illnesses are mostly caused by a shortage of proteins or vitamins. Symptoms of deficiency illnesses are

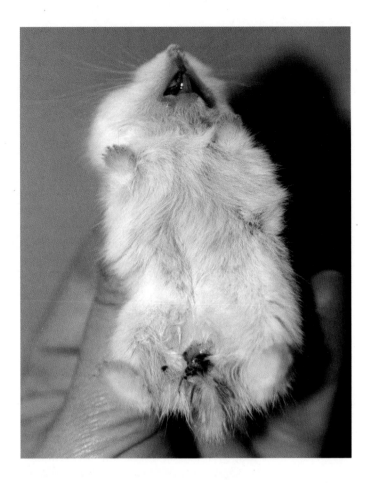

Dwarf hamster with diarrhea

problems with the skin or fur, poor growth, infertility, lowered resistance, and scabs around the nose. If dwarf hamsters get a varied diet, with enough nutrients and carbohydrates, the chances of deficiency illnesses are extremely small.

Wet tail

"Wet tail" is a very contagious hamster disease that is caused by a bacteria. Severe diarrhea, a lack of appetite, and lethargy, are the most important symptoms of this disease. Because of the diarrhea, the area around the tail becomes wet, and that is how the disease got its name. Wet tail is usually fatal. It seems that stress and hygiene can play an important role in the development of this illness because, of all them, badly cared for and stressed animals are the most susceptible. Because wet tail is extremely contagious, everything that the sick animal has been in contact with must be disinfected well.

A strong odor such as menthol or the smell of pines may cause allergic reactions

Digestive disorders

Dwarf hamsters can get diarrhea as a result of too many greens, contaminated drinking water, or incorrect housing (too cold, too drafty, or too damp). A dwarf hamster with diarrhea must be fed suitable meals for a while. Young ones can, mostly around the second week after their birth, suffer from constipation. Then they have a swollen, bluish belly, and have great difficulty in relieving themselves – sometimes they can't do this at all. This problem has to do with the changing over from their mother's milk to dry food. To prevent a shortage of moisture in the intestines, you should give young hamsters enough liquid and greens, for example, in the form of small pieces of apple. Constipation can also be the result of the wrong type of nesting material, or a lack of movement.

Infection of the bronchial tubes

Infections of the bronchial tubes are often caused by a bacteria that can strike when the bronchial tubes are weakened by a lack of ventilation or too damp or dusty living quarters. Just like human beings, dwarf hamsters can catch cold and show influenza-like symptoms complete with a sniffly, runny nose. You should put an animal that has any problems with its bronchial tubes in a warm, damp-free place. If it looks like the illness is getting worse, consult your veterinarian. Dwarf hamsters can also have a runny nose and watery eyes as a result of an allergy. The reasons can be too dusty an envi-

Russian dwarf hamster (left) and Campbell's dwarf hamster (right)

ronment, or a too strongly smelling floor covering, to which menthol or pine odors have been added.

Seizures

Some short-tailed dwarf hamsters can suffer from a kind of seizure. When they sit up straight, or jump up against

The muzzle must be clean

the walls of their quarters, they fall over on their backs, become somewhat convulsed, and scrabble themselves upright again. Nothing can be done about this strange illness. At the moment, it is not completely clear if this is a congenital defect or habitual compulsive behavior. In any case, it is advisable not to continue breeding with animals that have these sorts of seizures to any serious degree.

Old age

Older dwarf hamsters often become thinner. They lose their full coats, and start to walk more stiffly, with sunken flanks, and a crooked, arched back. Sometimes they suffer from fatty lumps, or long nails. Most old ones finally die in their sleep. With enough rest, sufficient comfortable nesting material, and a tasty morsel, you can usually ensure a very nice old age for your elderly dwarf hamster. Dwarf hamsters reach an average age of between one and a half and two years, with some exceptions that live to be three or four. The Chinese dwarf hamster usually lives somewhat longer than the Russian and Campbell's hamsters. The Roborovski hamster often does not live past its second birthday. If in a group of dwarf hamsters, a newborn one or an adult one dies, it can happen that the members of the group are busy clearing up the remains before you have the chance to do it yourself. Possibly you just find a bit of a skeleton, or a leftover bone, from the dead animal. This may not be nice for you to see, but this form of cannibalism in groups can't always be prevented.

Stay alert for the following symptoms and their possible causes.

Liquid feces – diarrhea, wet tail

No feces or difficulty in relieving themselves – constipation

Hard or swollen belly – constipation, pregnancy

Frequent urination – bladder or kidney problems, diabetes

Extreme thirst – bladder or kidney problems, diabetes

Hair loss – allergy, vermin, too little food

Frequent scratching – allergy, vermin, skin infection

Lumps – abscess (inflammation under the skin), tumor

Runny nose – allergy, common cold

Watery or sticky eyes – allergy, common cold, eye infection

Scabs – bite wounds, vermin

Apathy – overheating, shock, fever

Shivering – overheating, shock, fever, cold (inflammation of the lungs)

Sneezing – allergy, common cold

Weight loss – diabetes, tooth problems

Dribbling – overheating, tooth problems

Page 85:
Chinese dwarf
hamster baby

8 BREEDING
DWARF HAMSTERS

Primary considerations

Breeding dwarf hamsters is, in general, not very difficult, and before you know it, you have a whole set of them. If you are thinking it would be nice to breed dwarf hamsters, then, before you start, think about the fact that you will be the only one responsible for all those new young lives. So it is also sensible, before you start breeding, to look into whether there is enough interest in young dwarf hamsters, in your circle of friends, for example, or at your local pet specialty store. Make sure that you keep some cages or boxes in reserve, so that you can house the new increase in population in a responsible way.

Breeding short-tailed dwarf hamsters

Usually, breeding short-tailed dwarf hamsters proceeds without any problems. The best breeding results are achieved if the animals are kept in pairs.

There is a difference between fertility and "production" – some pairs never have offspring, while other pairs produce litter after litter like a production line, after which there may be a period without any babies. If the female is suckling

Close-up of a few-minutes-old dwarf hamster

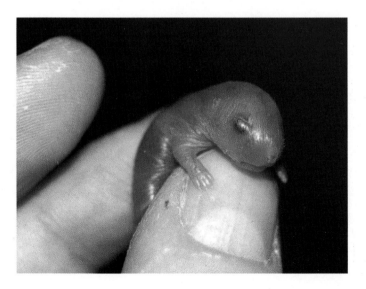

A family of dappled Campbell's dwarf hamsters

one set, she can already be pregnant with the next set. However, when the stream of new arrivals becomes too big, the mother can become stressed, and as a result, kill her own offspring. If this should happen, it is better to put the male and female in separate living quarters, so that no new litters arrive. But in such a case, take into account that a pair that has been separated from each other often cannot be reunited. Once you have gone through enough births, you can split your breeding group into males and females. With short-tailed dwarf hamsters, the fathers can live with their

Campbell's of a few days to a few weeks old

sons with no problems at all, and the mothers with their daughters. Apart from that, don't just put them with each other any old way, if they come from different cages, but use one or more tricks for this, as described in Chapter 3.

Seasonal?

In the wild, dwarf hamsters breed between April and September. Usually there then follow three or four litters, one after the other. In captivity, the litters are generally also born in the winter months. Russian and Campbell's dwarf hamsters that are born in the spring usually give birth to their first young in the summer of the same year. Roborovski dwarf hamsters are sometimes somewhat more difficult to breed. They often have their first litter only in the year following their birth, after the first winter of their lives. Because by then they are already a year old, and therefore, in dwarf hamster terms, are already elderly, the results of breeding the Roborovski dwarf hamster are often limited to just a few litters.

Breeding overview	
Length of pregnancy:	Russian dwarf hamster – 18-21 days
	Campbell's dwarf hamster – 16-18 days
	Roborovski dwarf hamster – 20-22 days
	Chinese dwarf hamster – 20-22 days
Sexually mature:	From the age of around 5 weeks
Fertile:	Once every 4 to 5 days
First litter:	Usually when they are around three months old
Number of babies:	1 to 12, average 4 to 6, but 6 to 7 quite regularly

Long-tailed – a completely different story

Breeding the long-tailed Chinese dwarf hamster is a completely different story. Because, as a rule, the females can be fairly aggressive compared to their male counterparts, breeding of this type is not as simple and matter-of-course as with the short-tailed variety. In laboratories, especially, various breeding methods have been tried. For example, the collar method, whereby the female hamster has a collar put around her neck, which prevents her from chasing the prospective father, and wounding it has been tried. Another method that has been tried is, with the aid of artificial light, the exchanging of day and night lighting, so that during the day the researchers can, during their working hours in the laboratory, have a good view of the behavior of

a pair of Chinese dwarf hamsters. It sometimes happens that a female Chinese dwarf is covered in the usual way, and that everything seems to be going well until she is actually pregnant. Then she can suddenly become out of sorts, and vent her emotions on the members of the present group. In such a case, it is, of course, a good idea to put the mother in separate living quarters, so that she can deliver her litter in peace. Together with her offspring, she can form a new breeding group because in practice it appears that reuniting her with the male after such an event is often no longer possible. However, because more and

Chinese dwarf hamster with his 16 day old son

A few minutes old, the muzzle is still rather bloody from biting through the membranes and umbilical cord

more breeders in the last few years have excluded too aggressive and too pugnacious animals from the breed, breeding Chinese hamsters has luckily become somewhat easier. So nowadays, breeding them is reasonably problem-free, as long as the owner knows what he or she is doing. However, when putting together each breeding pair, one still always has to wait and see how the female reacts to her partner.

Mottled Chinese dwarf hamsters
The mottled Chinese dwarf hamsters are, on average, more tolerant of each other than their naturally colored cousins.

Inbreeding or not?

If you want to start breeding dwarf hamsters, always keep in mind that you must start out with a number of healthy, adult animals, that have a good character. In principle, it can do no harm to inbreed dwarf hamsters over a number of generations—that is to say, crossbreeding a father and daughter, mother and son, or brother and sister, with each other. Sometimes inbreeding is actually necessary, to secure and conserve a particular characteristic (color). If you are a regular breeder, then it is sensible to crossbreed with non-related dwarf hamsters. The addition of "fresh" blood prevents degenerative symptoms, such as animals that are too small, less fertility, and congenital defects.

White red-eyed Campbell's with her few days-old youngster

Covering and the birth

A female dwarf hamster that is ready to mate presents herself to the male with a raised back and a raised tail. Then the paring ritual takes place a number of times. When dwarf hamsters are kept with each other, the person caring for them does not usually witness the covering, and only knows when the female has been covered when she is almost ready to give birth. A female dwarf hamster, especially, is only visibly plumper during the last days of pregnancy. During her pregnancy, she may eat extra concentrated tasty, nourishing snacks. It is a good idea not to disturb the mother during the birth. Any disturbance to the nest can cause her to drag the young somewhere else, out of pure stress, or even to kill and eat them. So it is a good idea, a few days before the expected birth, to make her quarters really clean—during the first two or three weeks after the birth, especially, you can't clean the accommodation, with the exception of the toilet corner, without the mother possibly becoming stressed, with all the consequences that this can have. Give her a sufficient amount of nesting material in advance, from which she can build a comfortable "delivery room." Because the mother hamster needs rest, you better not look into the delivery area to see if the birth has actually occurred. You can, of course, have a quick peek once the mother has left the nest. But you should control your curiosity. After about ten days, the young dwarf hamsters will crawl out of the nest by themselves, and then there is enough time to enjoy them. For that matter, you don't have to look to see what has happened in the nest at all – high squeaking will usually betray the fact that the young ones have been born.

Dwarf hamsters are born deaf, bald and blind

The father's role

In contrast to the case with longhaired hamsters (Chinese dwarf hamsters), the father of baby short-tailed dwarf hamsters will often remain in the nest. The father, and other hamsters that happen to be present, can play an important role in caring for the young, and especially in keeping them warm.

With the short-tailed dwarf hamsters the fathers help in bringing up the young

In practice, it appears that the chance of survival by the young is considerably less if the father animal is not present. But do make sure that the male has a separate place to sleep. It can happen sometimes that the mother can't bear him to be in the delivery area during the birth. Research has showed that Campbell's dwarf hamsters fulfill an extraordinary father's role. During their observations, Canadian researchers saw how the Campbell's males assisted during the birth, by biting through the umbilical cords, and licking the membranes open, among other things.

Development and rearing

Dwarf hamster babies develop extremely rapidly. After two days, the skin starts to get its color, and with the Russian, Campbell's and Chinese ones very small dorsal stripes can be seen. After this, the first hairs begin to show. Ten days after being born, the little ones have a complete coat of fur. Then they come out of the nest looking for solid food. When the young are about fourteen days old their eyes open. Whoever looks into the nest to follow these developments usually hears a cacophony of defensive squeaks. During the third and fourth weeks of life, the largest part of social development takes place. The little dwarf hamsters start to play, begin exploring their surroundings, and have

After a few days, the colors of these Campbell's are apparent: white red-eye, original color and black

fake fights. It is wonderful to see how they grow, and how they horse around. This is the moment to make the young dwarf hamsters familiar with humans. For this, get them used to your hands and your voice. But be careful because the young are still unruly, and very, very jittery – a paw can be broken just like that. After three weeks, the young hamsters can already go without their mother and her milk. However, they are then still too small to be able to stand up by themselves. So it is best to leave them with each other for another week or two. The little Roborovski dwarf hamster, especially, still needs the warmth of the nest. But, to prevent any unwanted offspring, keep the brothers with each other, and the sisters together in separate quarters. Only when a little dwarf hamster is at least five, but more likely, six weeks old, is it big enough, strong enough, and immune to stress enough, to leave its familiar surroundings and begin an independent life.

Ready to start a new life

9 COLOR AND FUR VARIETIES

Still more colors

For a considerable time, there were only naturally colored dwarf hamsters. Only in the last few decades have other colors appeared, especially with the Dwarf Russian and the Campbell's dwarf hamsters. In the future, there will undoubtedly be more colors added, which will make the hearts of dwarf hamster lovers beat faster—right now, all over the world, from the United States to Japan, new (color) varieties are appearing, and are being preserved by the enthusiasts.

The coat

A dwarf hamster's coat is often made up of different colors. You can easily see this by blowing on the coat in the opposite direction of how the hair is lying. The hairs separate from each other into the shape of a rosette, which makes them easy to inspect. The ends of the hairs on the head and back are sometimes of a darker color. The colored hair ends are also known together as the "ticking." Below this is the protective color. The lowest part of the hair, that grows closest to the skin, can sometimes be of a different color. This is the so-called ground or undercolor. The color of the underside of the animal is called the belly color. This can have an undercolor, but

Russian dwarf hamster, original color

no ticking. On the basis of the color descriptions in this chapter, you can try to find out what color your hamster is.

Fashion trends

Enthusiasts sometimes let themselves be blinded by the splendor of colors, and throw themselves with complete dedication into the "development" of new varieties. But they sometimes forget about what is really inside the skin of a dwarf hamster, the result being smaller and less healthy animals. There are often battles in the circle of enthusiasts to be the first to produce dwarf hamsters with a new color, but usually the novelty is already out of fashion after only one year. Dwarf hamster coloring is also especially susceptible to trends. One must realize that a dwarf hamster is more than just color. Physique, health, and character must always be the most important characteristics.

Russian dwarf hamster, blue-original color

Names of colors

Not only all over the world, but even in one country, colors are not always known by the same name. So the yellow-natural red-eyed Campbell's dwarf hamster is also sometimes called amber-gold or cinnamon, and there are breeders who themselves think up a (fantasy) name for a color, varying from snowflake to lavender. In addition, for a long time, people have been unable to agree on the origin of a color, or the way it is inherited. A choice has had to be made for this book, from the various naming conventions, and it has been decided to use the names and descriptions that are the most accepted by professional dwarf hamster breeders.

Dwarf Russian hamster colors

• Natural
The natural color is the original color of the Dwarf Russian hamster. Another name for this is agouti.

Coat color	gray-brown with black hair ends; undercolor dark slate blue
Belly color	(gray)white; undercolor dark blue
Dorsal stripe	brown-black to black
Triple-arch line	brown-black
Ears	dark, lighter on the inside
Eyes	black

• Blue-natural
The blue-natural Dwarf Russian hamster was discovered around 1988 in England. Its coat has a soft, smoky blue-gray tint. In the country of its origin, it is often referred to as "sapphire," named for the blue of the precious stone.

Coat color	blue-gray with a slightly purple bloom; undercolor dark blue
Belly color	off-white; undercolor blue
Dorsal stripe	blue
Triple-arch line	blue
Ears	dark gray, lighter on the inside
Eyes	black

• Pearl
The pearl (pearl-colored) Russian looks as if it is permanently in its winter coat—white, with dark shadows on the back, and especially on the head. This variety surfaced for the first time in England, around 1989.

Russian dwarf hamster, pearl

The pearl can be bred with both (white with black shadow), and blue-natural (white with blue shadow) colorings.

Coat color	white with light, even ticking
Belly color	pure white
Dorsal stripe	visible as a light shadow
Triple-arch line	sometimes still very vaguely visible
Ears	gray, lighter on the inside
Eyes	black

Until today, natural, blue-natural, and pearl were the only established color varieties of the Dwarf Russian hamster. Grey, dappled, albino, yellow-natural, and white-bellied Russian dwarf hamsters also appear on the market, but it is not clear if these are true purebred Russians, or crosses with Campbell's dwarf hamsters.

Campbell's dwarf hamster colors

• Self
The "Self" or agouti is the original color of the Campbell's dwarf hamster.

Left:
Campbell's,
original color

Right:
Campbell's,
yellow-original
color red-eye

Coat color	brown-yellow with darker brown hair ends, undercolor dark slate blue
Belly color	off-white, undercolor dark blue-gray
Dorsal stripe	dark brown
Triple-arch line	ochre brown to cream brown
Ears	dark, lighter on the inside
Eyes	black

• Argente
The yellow-natural is also called "argente." This variety was discovered in Moscow in 1979, and at the beginning of the nineties, came into the hands of the hamster lovers in Scandinavia, among others.

Coat color	warm yellow with a slight light brown wash, undercolor blue-gray
Belly color	ivory white; undercolor blue-gray
Dorsal stripe	brown
Triple-arch line	brown
Ears	flesh-colored
Eyes	red

• Black-eyed yellow-natural
The black-eyed yellow-natural is a variant with black eyes, that is slightly darker than the red-eyed type. This color is also called "sandy."

Coat color	brown-yellow with a gray undercolor
Belly color	off-white, undercolor gray
Dorsal stripe	dark gray
Triple-arch line	dark gray
Ears	gray
Eyes	black

• Opal
Not only the Russian dwarf hamster, but also the Campbell's dwarf hamster has a blue variant. With the Campbell's this is called "opal" (opal is a milky-white semiprecious stone, and also opal is the name for a blue breed of rabbits). The first opals, as far as is known, came from Canada, and came to Europe via the United States.

Right:
Campbell's, opal

Left:
Campbell's, albino

Coat color	blue-gray, undercolor dark gray
Belly color	ivory white
Dorsal stripe	blue-blue
Triple-arch line	blue-cream
Ears	gray
Eyes	black

• Albino
The first albino animals, also known as "red eyed," turned up in the middle of the eighties, and came to the west from Eastern Europe.

Coat color	clear white, with no markings or shading
Belly color	clear white
Ears	flesh-colored
Eyes	clear rose-red

• Black-eyed white
The white black-eyed Campbell's dwarf hamster is, as far as is known, the product of platinum in combination with dilute.

Coat color	pure white
Belly color	pure white
Ears	flesh-colored
Eyes	black

Left:
Campbell's, white
black-eye

Right:
Campbell's, black

• Black
The origins of the black Campbell's dwarf hamster are not completely certain. These animals have different appearances, from virtually completely black, to a somewhat lighter dark brown. The black dorsal stripe along the back is usually visible.

Coat color	as black as possible
Belly color	black
Dorsal stripe	black
Ears	flesh-colored to dark
Eyes	black

• Mottled

Mottled Campbell's dwarf hamsters have a varying amount of color and white. The pattern can vary enormously, from only a white neckband around the neck, to a whole host of white patches distributed evenly over the body. The first mottled Campbell's hamsters appeared in 1990 in England. The mottled hamsters can be bred in all sorts of colors.

Left:
Campbell's,
original color
spotted
Right:
Campbell's, black
spotted

Left:
Campbell's, black
with white
"neckband"
Right:
Campbell's, black
grey

Coat color	broken by a number of evenly spaces white patches
Belly color	white
Dorsal stripe	see the color concerned
Triple-arch line	see the color concerned
Ears	often mottled
Eyes	see the color concerned

• Platinum

The platinum factor causes the ends of the coat hairs to be white. Because of this, the actual color appears to be lighter—a sort of dappled effect. The amount of white

can vary, from just one white hair, to so many white ends that the animal appears to be virtually white.

• **Dilute**
Dilute is a dilution factor, whereby the color of the coat lightens, and so appears lighter than normal.

• **Umbrous**
Umbrous, the English word for "shady," is a darkening factor, that gives the color of a Campbell's dwarf hamster an extra, darker, tint.

Campbell's dwarf hamster's combination colors
Breeders are experimenting with the Campbell's colors to their heart's content. The crossbreeding of yellow-natural, opal and black, leads to an explosion of new color varieties. Yellow-natural red-eyed combined with opal, gives blue fawn (soft yellow with a blue tint, ivory-colored belly, blue-gray dorsal stripe, red eyes, and pink ears). Yellow-natural black-eyed, in combination with opal, gives lilac fawn (light yellow with a blue tint, ivory-colored belly, blue-gray dorsal stripe, black eyes, and gray ears).
Yellow-natural red-eyed, in combination with yellow-natural black-eyed, gives beige (yellow-beige with a brown dorsal stripe, red eyes, and gray ears). Yellow-natural red-eyed combined with yellow-natural black-eyed and opal, gives blue beige (beige with a blue tint, gray belly color, red eyes, and gray ears).
Black combined with opal gives blue (blue-gray topcoat, black eyes, and gray ears). Black in combination with yellow-natural black-eyed gives chocolate (chocolate brown topcoat, black eyes, and gray ears). Black combined with yellow-natural red-eyed gives dove gray (dove brown-brown coat, red eyes, and light-colored ears).
Black combined with yellow-natural black-eyed and opal gives lilac (soft lilac gray with black eyes and gray ears). Black in combination with yellow-natural red-eyed and opal gives lilac red-eyed (soft lilac gray with red eyes and flesh-colored ears). Black combined with yellow-natural black-eyed and yellow-natural red-eyed gives dark beige (dark beige with red eyes and flesh-colored ears). Finally, black combined with yellow-natural black-eyed, yellow-natural red-eyed and opal gives champagne (light beige with red eyes, and flesh-colored ears).

Left:
There is only
an original color
version of the
Roborovski

Right:
Chinese dwarf
hamster, original
color

Roborovski dwarf hamster coloring

• **Natural**
The Roborovski dwarf hamster is for the time being only
seen in its natural color (the color it is in the wild).

Coat color	dull sand yellow with a slight rust-brown sheen; undercolor slate blue
Belly color	pure white
Ears	flesh-colored, with dark-gray fur on the outside
Eyes	black
Markings	a white "eyebrow" above each eye

Chinese dwarf hamster coloring

• **Natural**
The original color of the Chinese dwarf hamster is natural (the color it has in the wild).

Coat color	brown-gray; undercolor dark slate gray
Belly color	white-white; undercolor dark blue
Dorsal stripe	black, reaching to the tail
Ears	dark with a lighter colored edge
Eyes	black

• **Dominant Spot**
In 1981, the Dominant Spot Chinese dwarf hamster appeared for the first time in England.

Coat color	broken by white spots, markings as symmetrical as possible
Belly color	clear white without undercolor

Dorsal stripe	may only be broken by white spots on the neck and on the head
Ears	dark with lighter colored edges or light spots
Eyes	black
Markings	for a show animal, a white spot on the skull is desirable

• **Black-eyed white**

The white Chinese dwarf hamster with black eyes was discovered in Switzerland. Now and then a black-eyed white, with or without a darker dorsal stripe, is born from Dominant Spot Chinese, but that has not yet led to stable breeding results. This color remains a matter of coincidence.

Coat color	pure white
Belly color	pure white
Ears	flesh-colored
Eyes	black

Other Chinese dwarf hamster colors

Every now and then, an albino Chinese dwarf hamster is born. Unfortunately, these animals are usually not viable. There are sometimes rumors going around about other colorings of this type of hamster, but there is little that is actually known.

Coat varieties

All types of dwarf hamsters have a normal shorthaired coat.

Right:
Chinese dwarf
hamster, spotted

Left:
Chinese dwarf
hamster, white
black-eye

Up until now, only with the Campbell's dwarf hamster are two deviating hair varieties known—the "satin" and the "wavy." The satin Campbell's dwarf hamster was discovered in England in 1981. Because the hairs of the satin variety's coat are hollow, the coat gets an extra strong and warm gloss. Because of this "satin" hair, the red-eyed white Campbell's dwarf hamster gets a some-what yellowish tint. The drawback is that because of the satin factor, the hairs are very fine and this makes them fall out quite often in small fatty tufts. Because of this, the satin effect doesn't always look very beautiful.

Since the nineties, "wavy" Campbell's have been in existence. These animals have a wavy coat, and often curly whiskers. Unfortunately, the curl usually disappears from the hair as the animal gets older. Now and then, there are Campbell's dwarf hamsters with a really curly coat (rex) or a longhaired coat, but for the time being they are extremely rare.

Hybrids

Unfortunately, crosses have been made and continue to be made between Russian and Campbell's dwarf hamsters. This is possible because these types have the same number of chromosomes (28). The young from this crossbreeding are called "hybrids." More breeding is done with these "Rusbellis" or "Camprussians." The result is that many dwarf hamsters of these types are no longer purebred. Many hybrids show the characteristics of both the Russian and Campbell's dwarf hamsters, for example, the black pigment of the Russian combined with the pointed head

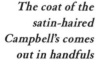

The coat of the satin-haired Campbell's comes out in handfuls

The dwarf hamster left has the blue color of the Russian, but in comparison with the pearl hamster bottom right, the muzzle and eyes of a Campbell's; the dappled dwarf hamster top right is a cross of a Russian and a Campbell's

of the Campbell's, or the browner color of the Campbell's in combination with the wide dorsal stripe of the Russian. However, it is not always visible from the outside that a dwarf hamster is a hybrid. Crossbreeding with Russian and Campbell's most happens through curiosity. For example, an attempt might be made to make the Russian dwarf hamster bigger, and to breed it with the coloring of the Campbell's. It can seem nice and tempting, but the crossing of Russians and Campbell's has a number of dangerous shortcomings. For example, due to the aggressive tendencies of the Campbell's, problems can arise with the character of the Russian dwarf hamster. In addition, the risk of health problems is great because illnesses and hereditary deviations can become transferred to the other type as a result of the crossbreeding. The crossbreeding of two types can also lead to lowered fertility. There can also be some nasty problems with the birth because Campbell's dwarf hamster young are larger and can't pass through the female Russian dwarf hamster's birth canal. So, in general, it is not adviseable to cross Russian dwarf hamsters with the Campbell's type. In the end it only results in problems – it could also mean the end of both types, and the characteristic properties of each type could also be lost through crossbreeding. In the wild, the Russian and Campbell's dwarf hamsters sometimes share the same habitat, although each type lives separately. For the rest, Chinese dwarf hamsters (22 chromosomes) and Roborovski dwarf hamsters (34 chromosomes) can't be crossed with other types of dwarf hamsters.

10 HEREDITY

Mutations

In nature, a certain number of natural-colored dwarf hamsters occur. So how can it be that the dwarf hamsters that live as pets come in so many different colors, markings, and types of fur? It all has to do with mutations. A new color, but also, for example, a different build, can come into being because of a spontaneous change to the hereditary make-up of a dwarf hamster—a mutation. A mutation can cause the pigmentation of the hair to change in form, or to become less in number, so that the color changes or becomes lighter. One example of a mutation is the albino Campbell's dwarf hamster. Mutations are hereditary. That means that some of the offspring of the albino can have the same deviating color as the father or mother animal. Sometimes a mutation can be an improvement, and can put a species in a better position to survive. If a white animal is born in a snowy habitat it will be seen and attacked less than the darker colored members of the same species and will therefore have more chance of survival. So the white animal will also get more opportunity to reproduce, and then a population can, slowly but surely, change in color, so that the species—albeit in a changed form—is able to survive. But, if such a white animal is born in a wooded environment, it becomes easy prey to predators. It will have a very small chance of survi-

The albino
Campbell's dwarf
hamster is
a mutation

val, let alone being able to reproduce. So the same mutation can turn out to be both positive and negative, depending on the environment in which the creature lives.

Establishing

Dwarf hamsters that are kept as pets have no natural enemies. As far as their chances of survival go, their color, or the length of their coats, makes no difference at all. Enthusiasts often try to establish mutations, and then go on breeding them, in the hope of creating a new variety. Mutations are freaks of nature. Whether or not a differently colored dwarf hamster suddenly appears in a litter is mostly a question of "wait and see," together with a certain amount of luck. Many mutations have appeared in laboratories, but that is not so strange because those are the places where breeding of rodents takes place on a large scale. The more breeding is done, the larger the number of animals, and with that, the greater the chance that a deviation (mutation) will occur.

Creation

A new color is not always the direct result of a mutation. By crossing colors, new colors can be created. In that case, we don't talk of a mutation, but of a combination or a creation. For example, crossing the yellow-natural (mutation) with a black (mutation), results in the dove-gray dwarf hamster (creation). Seen from the point of hereditariness, not all inheritable colors are also "real" colors. By cross-breeding animals of all sorts of colors, a mixture of vague intermediate colors can be created. For example, a black dwarf hamster that has too many brown tints, or a yellow one that is too orange can result. A breeder can dream up a beautiful new name for such a yellow-orange dwarf hamster, and say that he or she has created a new variety, but from the point of view of hereditariness, it just remains a yellow hamster, with a little too much orange in its color.

Genetics

To understand how colors are inherited, it is important to know something about genetics. Every animal carries hereditary information inside it, about a whole raft of characteristics, such as color and coat, but also character and build. This information is contained in the genes on the chromosomes that appear in every body cell. Young

dwarf hamsters receive this hereditary information part-ly from their father's sperm-cell, and partly from the mother's egg-cell, so in the case of its color, a "part" of the color. Colors are passed on according to a particular law. Some colors that are passed on are dominant, and others are subservient. For example, the original natural color of the Russian dwarf hamster is dominant, while the blue-natural color, on the other hand, is subservient. This means that a cross between a natural colored Russian dwarf ham-ster that only has natural colored ancestors, and a blue-nat-ural colored Russian dwarf hamster, will result in a litter

Campbell's dwarf hamster with filled cheek pouches

This blue-original color Russian has inherited the blue factor from both its father and its mother

of only natural colored offspring. The dominant natural color overrules the subservient blue color. But, the young dwarf hamsters that are born from this combination do carry the factor for the blue color in their hereditary material, albeit invisible to us. When the first generation are mutually crossbred, it can happen that the invisible bit of blue from the father animal "meets" the invisible bit of blue from the mother and results in the blue-natural coloring.

Formulas

For each color there is a genetic formula that is expressed by a letter code. For example, the color formula for the yellow-natural Campbell's dwarf hamster is "p." This stands for "pink-eyed dilution," a factor that dilutes the natural color towards yellow, and dilutes the black eye color towards red. The code for the pearl Russian dwarf hamster is Pe, the abbreviation of pearl. The code for the Dominant Spot Chinese dwarf hamster is Ds, standing for dominant spot.

Capital letters used in a genetic formula indicate that a color is a dominant one. Small letters mean that it is a subservient color. So the yellow-natural color (small letter p) is inherited by the Campbell's dwarf hamster as a subservient color. Pearl (Pe), on the other hand, is inherited by the Russian dwarf hamster as a dominant color. From the genetic color formula, one can also see from

With the Campbell's, yellow-original color is recessive relative to the original color

what other colors a color has been created. So the dove-gray Campbell's dwarf hamster, a combination of the colors black (aa) and yellow-natural (pp), has the formula aapp, and the champagne Campbell's dwarf hamster, consisting of a combination of preferably four different colors (black, yellow-natural black-eyed, yellow-natural red-eyed, and opal), has the formula aabbppdd.

With the Russian, pearl is dominant relative to the original color

Genetic symbols of mutations occurring in dwarf hamsters

- **Russian dwarf hamster:**

Blue-natural	d
Pearl	Pe

- **Campbell's dwarf hamster:**

Albino	c
Yellow-natural red-eyed	p
Yellow-natural black-eyed	b
Opal	d
Black	a
Umbrous	u
Mottled	Mo
Platinum	Si
Satin-haired	sa
Wavy	wa

- **Chinese dwarf hamster:**

Dominant spot	Ds
Black-eyed white	Ws

Purebred stock

A very frequently asked question from both beginners and experienced breeders is, "What do I get if I cross color X with color Y?" The answer to this question depends on whether the animal is of purebred stock or not. An animal of purebreed stock is also called a homozygote. This means that it does not carry any other color than that which can be seen on the outside. One that is not pure breeding stock, or heterozygote, can, without anything being visible on the outside, be carrying other colors. The following is an example: We cross a natural (Self) Campbell's dwarf hamster with a black (aa) Campbell's dwarf hamster. Only natural colored offspring are born. From this we can deduce that the natural parent is of purebred stock (AA). Because the natural color passed on is dominant, and the black subservient, in this case only natural colored babies are born, that

Black Campbell's

do, however, all carry the hereditary factor for black (Aa, whereby they have received the A from one of the parent animals, and the a from the other one). If we now crossbreed these babies (Aa x Aa), homozygote natural-colored (AA), heterozygote natural-colored animals that are carrying the black factor (Aa), and black dwarf hamsters (aa) can be born. From the outside we can't see whether the offspring are pure breeding stock or not. For these animals, we use the code A-, where the minus sign means that the animal can be either AA (natural-colored pure breeding stock), or Aa (natural-colored heterozygote).

Now we cross another natural-colored Campbell's dwarf hamster with a black (aa) Campbell's. In this case there are both natural-colored and black babies born. From this we can tell that the natural-colored parent is not pure breeding stock (Aa), and, hidden under its dominant, natural-colored coat, it is carrying the subservient black factor. The peculiarity of a subversive inherited property is that it can be passed on for generations without ever appearing, and then "suddenly" appear when two animals are paired with each other, that both, by coincidence, are carrying this property.

Calculating the odds

How many animals of a particular color or variety are born is a question of calculating the odds. Suppose you cross a satin-haired Campbell's dwarf hamster with a normal dwarf hamster. Satin hair is inherited as a subservient factor. The normal-haired dwarf hamster appears not to carry any satin factor, so 100% normal haired dwarf hamsters are born that all carry the satin factor.

If we now cross the animals with each other, then there is a 25% chance of normal haired offspring that do not carry the satin factor, a 50% chance of normal haired ones that do carry the satin factor, and a 25% chance of satin hamsters being the result. If you cross a normal haired Campbell's, carrying the satin factor, with a satin-haired one, there is a 50% chance of the young being normal-haired, but carrying the satin factor, and a 50% chance of them being satin-haired. If you cross

Both white, but resulting from a different factor; left: a white black-eye Campbell's; right: a red-eye

a satin-haired hamster with another satin one, then there is a 100% certainty that the babies will also be satin.

Calculations

The more color factors are involved, the more complicated the calculation of the odds becomes. Suppose you cross-breed a natural Campbell's hamster, that carries the black factor, with an opal Campbell's dwarf hamster that carries the red-eyed yellow-natural factor. According to the rules

A natural-color Russian and a somewhat gray variant; a new color perhaps?

for calculating the odds, you can expect the litter to be as follows – 12.5% natural-colored animals of pure breeding stock, 12.5% natural animals that carry the opal factor, 12.5% natural ones that carry the red-eyed yellow-natural factor, 12.5% natural that carry both the opal and the red-eyed yellow-natural factor, 12.5% natural that carry the black factor, 12.5% natural that carry both black and opal factors, 12.5% natural that carry the black and the red-eyed yellow-natural factors, and 12.5% natural colored animals that carry the black, opal, and red-eyed yellow-natural factors. In short, all natural-colored homozygous animals (of which can't be seen from the outside) and

Young dwarf hamster

which may inherit other colors. So breeding always remains a bit of a gamble.

Sometimes you can work out precisely what to expect. If two natural Campbell's dwarf hamsters are crossed, of which you know that both are carrying the black, red-eyed yellow-natural, and opal factors, then, according to the rules, you can calculate the chances of natural, black, red-eyed yellow-natural, opal, blue, dove gray, blue fawn and red-eyed lilac according to the ratio 27:9:9:9:3:3:3:1. In practice, it appears that these complicated calculations based on large numbers do not always turn out that way. As you can see from the ratio, the chance of natural color is very high, and the chance of red-eyed lilac, at 1 to 64, very small.

In order to breed a subservient inheritable color, both of the parents must have that color or be carrying it in their genetic material. With dominant hereditary colors this is not the case—only one of the parents has to have the color for young to be born of that color. So you only need one pearl Russian dwarf hamster to start breeding pearl Russian dwarf hamsters. The combination of pearl times natural, according to the calculation of the odds, gives you 50% pearl and 50% natural. Because pearl is a dominant factor, pearls can never be born from two natural-colored animals.

Deviations

Some color genes appear to be linked to a lessened viability or fertility. So it appears that Russian dwarf hamster young, from the combination blue-natural and blue-natural, are not always

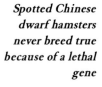

Spotted Chinese dwarf hamsters never breed true because of a lethal gene

viable, and the pearl Russian dwarf hamster is sometimes less fertile. With the black-eyed Chinese dwarf hamsters that now and then appear, the males have an underdeveloped scrotum, and are sterile (infertile). The genetic code for this color is Ws, standing for "White and sterile."

Some marking patterns, as a result of a so-called homozygote lethal factor, can't be bred in a form that makes for pure breeding stock. This is the case, for example, with the mottled Campbell's dwarf hamster. Whoever crosses two mottled animals with each other, runs the risk that the litter will contain some young that are not viable, completely white and eyeless, that mostly die shortly after being born. However, the combination of mottled and mottled can be avoided, seeing that mottled is passed on as a dominant factor, so that the combination mottled with natural (or another color) also results in mottled offspring.

We also find the same lethal factor in the Dominant Spot Chinese dwarf hamster. In this case, the homozygote animals (DsDs) are not born, but die very early in the womb. Dominant Spot Chinese dwarf hamsters are therefore, by definition, heterozygotes (Dsds). This means that from two Dominant Spot animals, natural-colored animals (dsds) can always be born. Dominant Spot bred with Dominant Spot gives 50% Dominant Spot that are not pure breeding stock, 25% natural and 25% Dominant Spot that are breeding stock (these last ones are not born, so the litters from this combination can be smaller than usual). Dominant Spot crossed with natural gives 50% Dominant Spot and 50% natural. The spotted pattern of the Chinese dwarf hamster is passed on as dominant, which means that Dominant Spot offspring can never be born from the mating of two natural-colored Chinese.

11 THE IDEAL DWARF HAMSTER

To the show

Shows are organized in many countries where specially trained judges judge dwarf hamsters as to their outward appearance. At such a show, you can acquire experience, and meet a lot of other enthusiasts. Maybe you'll also find it nice to register your own dwarf hamsters for such an inspection. Dwarf hamster inspections take place at pet exhibitions, where other animals, such as rabbits and poultry, can also be seen.

In principle, it doesn't really matter where your dwarf hamster comes from, if you want to join in a show. Sport breeders pay attention to the exterior of the animals, and make their choices heavily based on this, but it is possible that your "simple" dwarf hamster from the pet store also has an appearance that is suitable for these inspections. So if there is a "top class" hidden away in your dwarf hamster, it is just a question of trying!

Handling

For such an inspection, dwarf hamsters must be easy to handle and to look at, and this is sometimes a problem

*Small hamsters
win small prizes*

with the Campbell's dwarf hamster and the Roborovski. The Campbell's can be somewhat moody, and the fast Robby almost never sits still for a second. Pretty or not-so-pretty, all dwarf hamsters that appear for showing must be clean, healthy, and in good condition. Sick and visibly pregnant animals are excluded from the awards, as are Russian dwarf hamsters in their winter coat. Animals with wounds, torn ears, bald patches and vermin, are also not considered for prizes. Too old or too young animals are also not suitable for showing.

Points that are looked out for when inspecting a dwarf hamster	
Type and build	Head, eyes, and ears
Size	Color and marking pattern
Coat	Condition

Standard and breed description

To be able to judge dwarf hamsters from their exterior, an official standard has been drawn up, in which it is precisely stated which requirements the animals must satisfy. These requirements can differ from one country to another. For some types of dwarf hamsters, no standard has yet been laid down, nor are all the colors recognized. Each country has its own assessment committee that decides about any possible recognition of a type or a variety. The breed description for each type of dwarf hamster can also differ from country to country. Most of the differences have to do with body length

and body weight. It is noticeable that many show animals are a little heavier than their wild brothers and sisters. The weight of a Russian dwarf hamster in the wild can be around 25 grams, while some show animals weigh three times as much! The following paragraphs give you a global description of how each type ought to look, in general terms.

Russian dwarf hamster

The ideal Russian dwarf hamster is almost spherical in shape. It has a body length of between 7 and 10 centimeters, and a tail that is between 0.5 and 1 centimeter long, and is hardly visible. Its weight is somewhere around 45 to 50 grams. The fur must be close, fine and soft, and have a thick undercoat. The fur is glossy and full, and gives the impression of wool. The head of a Russian dwarf hamster is broad and blunt with good cheeks, and a somewhat Roman curved nose. The eyes are round and spherical in form. The ears must be small and round.

Campbell's dwarf hamster

The Campbell's dwarf hamster should be sturdy and robust in structure, and have a body length of between 8 and 12 centimeters. The tail is between 0.5 and 1 centimeter long. Its weight is somewhere around 50 to 60 grams. The Campbell's dwarf hamster's fur is close and tight. The fur is glossy and full. The head comes slightly to a point, but the Campbell's dwarf hamster's muzzle must not be too pointed. The eyes are round, and the ears reasonably small and round.

Left:
Blue original - color Russian dwarf hamster with the requisite round conformation being inspected by the judge

Right:
Campbells wait in their show cage to be judged at a British show

Right:
Roborovski dwarf
hamsters are
difficult to judge
because they are
so quick

Left:
The head of the
Chinese dwarf
hamster is
somewhat
triangular in
shape

Roborovski dwarf hamster

The Roborovski dwarf hamster is small, but plump in build, with a nice round shape. It has a body length from about 5 centimeters long, but on average is about 7 centimeters. The tail is around 0.5 centimeters long and almost invisible. It weighs between 30 and 40 grams on average. The Roborovski dwarf hamster has a full coat. Its fur stands slightly open, whereby the blue undercolor can be seen. The head is slightly tapered, but not pointed. The whiskers are strongly developed. The eyes are large, round, and spherical in shape. A Roborovski has reasonably large ears that are rounded in shape at the top.

Chinese dwarf hamster

The Chinese dwarf hamster has a moderately stretched body. It has a regular and slightly slim build, with nice curves. This dwarf hamster has a length of between 9 and 12 centimeters, and a tail that is between 2 and 2.5 centimeters long. Its weight is between 40 grams for females, and 45 grams for males, that are somewhat bigger and especially longer. The coat is fine and soft in structure, and should be thick and lie flat on the skin. The head of the Chinese dwarf hamster is broad with good cheeks. The lines between the ears and the tip of the nose form a sort of triangle. The eyes are round and spherical in shape. The ears are not too large and are rounded at the top.

The judging

The dwarf hamsters travel to shows in small transport boxes, or show cages. All the cages are numbered, and then placed on tables, in the order of their classes. The judge then takes the hamsters out of their boxes or cages, one by one, and places them on a grating or a piece of floor covering to judge them against their breed standard. Not only are the strong points of each dwarf hamster noted on the evaluation card, but also the weak points, such as too little hair on the belly, for example, a color deviation, or an irregular dorsal stripe on the back. The judge assigns the registered dwarf hamsters a number of points, or a designation. The ones with the best scores have the chance of being the best of their variety or the best of their type. For the winners there are small cash prizes, rosettes, medals, and cups. To bring your dwarf hamster into peak condition for a show, a little bit before the day of judging, you can give it an extra amount of hay, peanuts, sunflower seeds, and a sand bath. This provides an extra shine on the coat. In addition, it goes without saying that a show animal's nails and teeth must be cared for, and in good condition. During a competition, you can generally always talk to other enthusiasts, and get good advice and/or breeding material. You'll meet people who are completely under the spell of the dwarf hamster. They will virtually all have started with one animal, but, in the meantime, only as a hobby, they have expanded to maybe more than one hundred of these endearing balls of fur. Look out because the dwarf hamster enthusiasm virus is very contagious!

The thin dorsal stripe of the Campbell's (left) and the broader dorsal stripe of the Russian; both dorsal stripes are rather too short, they should run right through to the tail

The author taking part in a dwarf hamster judging in Great Britain

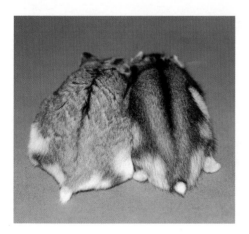

Important addresses

Associations
California Hamster Association
23651 Dune Mear, Lake Forrest, CA 92630

Brittish Hamster Association
PO BOX 825, Sheffield, S 173RU, UK

Internet
A lot of information about (dwarf) hamsters can be found on the internet. One site with an enormous amount of up-to-date information is Lorraine Hill's "The Complete Hamster Site" in England. The address is http://www.petwebsite.com/hamsters.htm. Those who would like to know more about the inheritance of colors as regards the Campbell's dwarf hamster, can find a very extensive overview in words and pictures on the Heavenly Hamsters website in the United States. The address is http://www.heavenlyhamsters.com/campbellgenetics.htm

THANKS
AND PHOTO CREDITS

The author would like to thank all the enthusiasts and breeders who were friendly enough to allow their dwarf hamsters to be photographed, and to provide useful information, especially Chris Henwood, Lorraine Hill, and Pamela Milward. Special thanks to Esther Verhoef for the pleasant assistance and collaboration.

All the advice and information in this book has been carefully chosen by the author, and, as far as possible, is scientifically based on, and verified against, the latest information, by studying various sources. Nevertheless, neither the author nor the publisher can be held responsible for any consequences of following this advice.

All photographs were taken by Judith Lissenberg, with the exception of those on pages 6, 13 bottom, 104 left and 125 right, which were taken by Esther Verhoef for FurryTails.nl.